POLICY RESEARCH IN
EDUCATIONAL SETTINGS

DOING QUALITATIVE RESEARCH IN EDUCATIONAL SETTINGS

Series Editor: Pat Sikes

The aim of this series is to provide a range of high quality introductory research methods texts. Each volume focuses, critically, on one particular methodology enabling a detailed yet accessible discussion. All of the contributing authors are established researchers with substantial, practical experience. While every book has its own unique style, each discusses the historical background of the approach, epistemological issues and appropriate uses. They then go on to describe the operationalization of the approach in educational settings drawing upon specific and vivid examples from the authors' own work. The intention is that readers should come away with a level of understanding that enables them to feel sufficiently confident to undertake their own research as well as to critically evaluate other accounts of research using the approach.

Published titles

Michael Bassey: *Case Study Research in Educational Settings*
Morwenna Griffiths: *Educational Research for Social Justice*
Jenny Ozga: *Policy Research in Educational Settings*

POLICY RESEARCH IN EDUCATIONAL SETTINGS

Contested terrain

Jenny Ozga

Open University Press
Buckingham · Philadelphia

Open University Press
Celtic Court
22 Ballmoor
Buckingham
MK18 1XW

e-mail: enquiries@openup.co.uk
world wide web: http://www.openup.co.uk

and

325 Chestnut Street
Philadelphia, PA 19106, USA

First Published 2000

A catalogue record of this book is available from the British Library

ISBN   0 335 20295 0 (pb)   0 335 20296 9 (hb)

Library of Congress Cataloging-in-Publication Data
Ozga, Jennifer.
     Policy research in educational settings: contested terrain /
Jenny Ozga.
          p.   cm. – (Doing qualitative research in educational settings)
     Includes bibliographical references and indexes.
     ISBN 0-335-20296-9 (hb). – ISBN 0-335-20295-0 (pb)
     1. Education–Research–Great Britain–Methodology.   2. Education
and state–Research–Great Britain–Methodology.   3. Action research
in education–Great Britain.   4. Critical pedagogy–Great Britain.
     I. Title.   II. Series
     LB1028.25.G7O93   1999
     370'.7'2–dc21   99-24211
                                                                                               CIP

Typeset by Type Study, Scarborough
Printed in Great Britain by Biddles Ltd, Guildford and King's Lynn

For Tadeusz Antoni Ozga, 1919–1996

Contents

Series editor's preface

I had never realized just how fascinating research was in its own right. I was expecting the research methods course to be boring, difficult and all about statistics but I couldn't have been more wrong. There is so much to consider, so many aspects, so many ways of finding out what's going on, and not just one way of representing it too. I have been really surprised.

(Student taking an MA in Educational Studies)

I never knew that there was so much to research. I thought that you just chose a method, applied it, did your statistical sums and came up with your findings. The reality is more complicated but so much more interesting and meaningful.

(Student taking an MA in Educational Studies)

The best thing for me was being told that qualitative research is 'proper' research – providing it's done properly of course. What goes on in schools is so complex and involves so many different perspectives that I think you often need a qualitative approach to begin to get some idea of what's going on.

(Student taking an MA in Sociology)

I really appreciate hearing about other researchers' experiences of doing research. It was quite a revelation when I first became aware that things don't always go as smoothly as some written accounts seem to suggest. It's really reassuring to hear honest reports: they alert you to pitfalls and problems and things that you might not have thought about.

(Doctoral student)

Comments such as these will be familiar to anyone who has ever taught or taken a course which aims to introduce the range of research approaches available to social scientists in general and those working in educational settings in particular.

The central message that they convey seems to be that the influence of the positivist scientist paradigm is both strong and pervasive, shaping expectations of what constitutes 'proper', 'valid' and 'worthwhile' research. What Barry Troyna wrote in 1994, continues to be the case; namely that:

> There is a view which is already entrenched and circulating widely in the populist circles ... that qualitative research is subjective, value-laden and, therefore, unscientific and invalid, in contrast to quantitative research, which meets the criteria of being objective, value-free, scientific and therefore valid.
>
> (1994: 9)

Within academic and research circles though, where the development of post-modernist and post-structuralist ideas have affected both thinking and research practice, it can be easy to forget what the popular perspective is. This is because, in these communities, qualitative researchers from the range of theoretical standpoints utilize a variety of methods, approaches, strategies and techniques in the full confidence that their work is rigorous, legitimate and totally justifiable as research. And the process of peer review serves to confirm that confidence.

Recently, however, for those concerned with and involved in research in educational settings, and especially for those engaged in educational research, it seems that the positivist model, using experimental, scientific, quantitative methods, is definitely in the ascendancy once again. Those of us working in England and Wales go into the new millennium with the government endorsed exhortation to produce evidence-based research that,

> (firstly) demonstrates conclusively that if teachers change their practice from x to y there will be significant and enduring improvement in teaching and learning; and (secondly) has developed an effective method of convincing teachers of the benefits of, and means to, changing from x to y.
>
> (Hargreaves 1996: 5)

If it is to realize its commendable aims of school effectiveness and school improvement research, as portrayed here, demands 'objectivity', experiments and statistical proofs. There is a problem with this requirement though and the essence of it is that educational institutions and the individuals who are involved in and with them are a heterogeneous bunch with different attributes, abilities, aptitudes, aims, values, perspectives, needs and so on. Furthermore, these institutions and individuals are located within complex social contexts with all the implications and influences that this entails. On its own, research whose findings can be expressed in mathematical terms is unlikely to be sophisticated enough to sufficiently accommodate and account for the myriad differences that are involved. As one group of prominent educational researchers has noted:

We will argue that schooling does have its troubles. However, we maintain that the analysis of the nature and location of these troubles by the school effectiveness research literature, and in turn those writing Department for Employment and Education policy off the back of this research, is oversimplified, misleading and thereby educationally and politically dangerous (notwithstanding claims of honourable intent).

(Slee *et al.* 1998: 1–9)

There is a need for rigorous research which does not ignore, but rather addresses, the complexity of the various aspects of schools and schooling: for research which explores and takes account of different objective experiences and subjective perspectives, and which acknowledges that qualitative information is essential, both in its own right and also in order to make full and proper use of quantitative indicators. The *Doing Qualitative Research in Educational Settings* series of books is based on this fundamental belief. Thus the overall aims of the series are: to illustrate the potential that particular qualitative approaches have for research in educational settings; and to consider some of the practicalities involved and issues that are raised when doing qualitative research so that readers will feel equipped to embark on research of their own.

At this point it is worth noting that qualitative research is difficult to define as it means different things at different times and in different contexts. Having said this, Denzin and Lincoln's (1994) generic definition offers a useful starting point:

Qualitative research is multimethod in focus, involving an interpretive, naturalistic approach to its subject matter. This means that qualitative researchers study things in their natural settings, attempting to make sense of, or interpret, phenomena in terms of the meanings people bring to them. Qualitative research involves the studied use and collection of a variety of empirical materials . . . that describe routine and problematic moments and meanings in individuals' lives. Accordingly, qualitative researchers deploy a wide range of interconnected methods, hoping always to get a better fix on the subject matter at hand.

(Denzin and Lincoln 1994: 2)

The authors contributing to the series are established, well-known researchers with a wealth of experience on which to draw and all make use of specific and vivid examples from their own and others' work. A consequence of this use of examples is the way in which each writer conveys a sense of research being an intensely satisfying and enjoyable activity, in spite of the specific difficulties that are sometimes encountered.

Whilst they differ in terms of structure and layout each book deals with:

• The historical background of the approach: how it developed; examples of its use; implications for its use at the present time.

- Epistemological issues: the nature of the data produced; the roles of the researcher and the researched.
- Appropriate uses: in what research contexts and for which research questions is the approach most appropriate; where might the research be inappropriate or unlikely to yield the best data.

They then describe it and discuss using the approach in educational settings, looking at such matters as:

- How to do it: designing and setting up the research; planning and preparation; negotiating access; likely problems; technical details; recording of data.
- Ethical considerations: the roles of and the relationship between the researcher and the researched; ownership of data; issues of honesty.
- Data analysis.
- Presentation of findings: issues to do with writing up and presenting findings.

Jenny Ozga's book, *Policy Research in Educational Settings: Contested Terrain*, is firmly located within a political context in which much educational policy appears to be shaped by, and oriented towards, the economizing and marketization of education. An important consequence of this trend is the depoliticization of citizens who become uncritical 'consumers', 'clients' and 'technicians' in a globalized, post-Fordist society. As a check on this, Jenny argues for educational practitioners of all kinds (teachers, Local Education Authority advisers, etc.), researchers and academics to engage in research which can provide them with an informed, critical, independent and authoritative base to speak against misguided, mistaken and unjust educational policy.

The development and improvement of all aspects of education for everyone should be, and no doubt is, the avowed and ultimate aim of policy makers and researchers alike. However, what counts as development and improvement is not necessarily unproblematic and universal. Thus, Jenny suggests that the perspective which appears to be to seek to limit educational research to the strictly useful gives rise to the fundamental question, in *whose* interests and for *what* purpose should such research be done? It is in order to address this question that teachers should themselves take a critical and reflexive approach to policy.

In line with this view, Jenny stresses that there is no fixed, single definition of policy but rather advocates seeing it as a process which involves contestation and negotiation between different groups. These groups may not actually be officially involved in policy making: teachers' various realizations of aspects of the 1988 Educational Reform Act and pupils' responses to these enactments are a graphic illustration of this.

Policy Research in Educational Settings: Contested Terrain makes extensive use of examples in putting a strong case for teachers and other educational practitioners to take a research-based approach to their work *per se*, seeing them as crucial participants in policy making. It is, therefore, a book for everyone concerned in the educational enterprise rather than simply for those who are engaged in 'research' for whatever purpose.

Final note

It was Barry Troyna who initially came up with the idea for this series. Although his publishing career was extensive, Barry had never been a series editor and, in his inimitable way, was very keen to become one. Whilst he was probably best known for his work in the field of 'race', Barry was getting increasingly interested in issues to do with methodology when he became ill with the cancer which was eventually to kill him. It was during the twelve months of his illness that he and I drew up a proposal and approached potential authors. All of us knew that it was very likely that he would not live to see the series in print but he was adamant that it should go ahead, nonetheless. The series is, therefore, something of a memorial to him and royalties from it will be going to the Radiotherapy Unit at the Walsgrave Hospital in Coventry.

Pat Sikes

References

Denzin, N. and Lincoln, Y. (1994) Introduction: entering the field of qualitative research. In N. Denzin and Y. Lincoln (eds) *Handbook of Qualitative Research*. California: Sage.

Hargraves, D. (1996) Teaching as a research-based profession: possibilities and prospects. Tearcher Training Agency Annual Lecture. London: TTA.

Slee, R. and Weiner, G. with Tomlinson, S. (eds) (1998) Introduction: school effectiveness for whom? In *School Effectiveness for Whom? Challenges to the School Effectiveness and School Improvement Movements*. London: Falmer.

Troyna, B. (1994) Blind faith? Empowerment and educational research, *International Studies in the Sociology of Education*, 4(1): 3–24.

Acknowledgements

I would like to thank all those who have helped me with this book, through the process of 'constructive conversations'; some of them over many years, some of them more recent. Responsibility for the outcomes of these conversations as reported here is, of course, all mine. Some of the less constructive conversations have also, inadvertently, contributed to the book, but I don't think those should be acknowledged. My thanks, then, go to current and former colleagues, notably Barbara Cole, Roger Dale, Rosemary Deem, Ross Fergusson, Sharon Gewirtz, Helen Gunter, Ken Jones, Martin Lawn, Monica McLean, David Pye, Farzana Shain, Laura Sukhnandan and Lynne Walker. Thanks also go to more distant sources of illumination, in particular to Terri Seddon, but also to Jill Blackmore and Jane Kenway. I should also acknowledge my debt to students on the Open University's course 'Policy making in Education', and on the policy elements of Keele University's undergraduate programme in educational studies. Thanks for technical and human support go to Carol Hough and Gladys Pye. Finally, my thanks go to Anita West and Shona Mullen at Open University Press, and to Pat Sikes, the series editor, for their patience.

1 | Researching education policy: some arguments

Introduction: policy research as contestation

This book is about doing educational research in 'policy settings'; that is, in places, processes and relationships where policy is made. I have subtitled it 'contested terrain' for two reasons: first, because I want to make it clear that my understanding of policy is that it is struggled over, not delivered, in tablets of stone, to a grateful or quiescent population; second, to signal the current conflict in the field of research on education policy. Throughout the book I shall be trying to contribute to an argument in favour of the informed, independent contestation of policy by a research community of teachers and academics who have together developed capacities that allow them to speak with authority against misguided, mistaken and unjust education policy. I shall try to set out some of the ways in which it is possible to think about, design and carry out investigations of education policy that contribute to that overall project, and I shall discuss some of the trends in the current policy context and in policy direction that make that task urgent and necessary. In particular, I shall consider the impact of recent policy on the teaching profession, and on its capacity to contribute to, and benefit from, research.

It should be clear that this is not a research handbook or a methodological primer, although there will be some discussion of resources available to researchers on education policy, and some exemplification of different methodological approaches and choices. The discussion of methodologies should be understood as part of the overall argument about contestation of 'official' policy, and not as something separate and technical; my point is that the orientation of a policy researcher towards a policy problem is likely to have consequences for the kinds of investigation that she or he carries out. So I am not concerned here to set out a comprehensive display of research methods; instead, I consider how different theoretical approaches connect to different methods of enquiry and analysis.

A major issue is what is meant by the term 'policy'. I discuss different ways of defining policy in Chapter 3, but for now I want to stress that there is no fixed, single definition of policy. How the term is understood depends to a considerable degree on the perspective of the researcher. There are those who understand policy in quite straightforward terms as the actions of government, aimed at securing particular outcomes. I take a rather different, more diffuse view of policy as a *process* rather than a product, involving negotiation, contestation or struggle between different groups who may lie outside the formal machinery of official policy making. I try to make this argument clearer by dealing with the relationship between teachers and policy making as a core topic of the book.

Although this is not a handbook, or a guide to how to do policy research, I hope that it will stimulate interest in policy research in education, and encourage more people to engage in it. The broad, process-oriented definition of policy that I argue for is also helpful in making 'policy research' more accessible, because it extends the possibilities for research beyond the formal mechanisms of government – where access may be difficult, and beyond policy developments at the macro system level. Policy research can be done within institutions or classrooms, as well as within local education authorities or government departments. Such research can act as a commentary or critique of 'official' research outputs, and assist those who implement or mediate policy to orient themselves in relation to official research claims; for example, in relation to class size, or setting, or the operation of choice of school, college or university.

I believe that a stronger engagement with policy research in education would help to inhibit the misuse or simplification of research by policymakers, who denigrate or ignore research that does not support their chosen policy direction, while claiming to be committed to 'evidence-based policy making'. I want to encourage a wide range of people to become involved in research in education policy. I want to remove 'policy' from its pedestal, and make it accessible to the wider community, both as a subject of study and as a possible research area. In doing this I am arguing – implicitly and explicitly – that policy is to be found everywhere in education, and not just at the level of central government, and that there is virtue in engaging with policy in this way, because it contributes to a democratic project in education, which in turn contributes to democracy as the creation of an informed, active citizenry, supported, as Dewey (1916) imagined, by an informed, activated system of public education.

Because I am working within that framework of ideas, the book concentrates on teachers and educationalists, and on the ways in which education policy research can enhance their capacity for producing such an informed, activated system of education that in turn creates an informed citizenry. But I do not wish to exclude others in education or with an interest in education from the policy research field. Indeed, it could be argued, in my view, that all research in education to some degree engages with policy. It is difficult to imagine an education research project that takes place 'outside' policy. So there is very considerable scope for work in this area, in many different ways. For example, parents may be involved in research on policy when they investigate the processes and consequences of choice of school for their child. They may rapidly become involved in the examination of evidence that takes them into issues of policy and beyond the 'straightforward' issue of choice. Definitions of choice, assessment of benefit, consequences for the locality, local procedures and policies all become part of the picture, and an assessment of your child's needs may be readily reformulated as a comparative study of educational provision, or of teacher–parent relationships, or of school management styles.

School choice is obviously a policy issue: it is a slogan that encapsulates formal government policy as pursued by the last Conservative administration in England; it is an issue that raises interesting questions in relation to responsibility for policy in a local area; and it is a meeting point between that public policy world and the private world of personal choice, preferences and identities. I look at research on school choice on a number of occasions in the book. But there are other ways in which policy is accessible and apparent in our immediate contexts, and not only at an abstract or remote level. Teachers are policy makers: they have a strong influence on the interpretation of policy, and they engage with policy at a number of levels, from the national level of formal policy making through to the informal arena of pupil–teacher relations.

Pupils, too, may be understood as policy makers; for example, if they become involved in making use of formal mechanisms of policy for their school (instances are equal opportunities or anti-bullying policy). My point is that policy as a subject of research is available to a wide audience and, furthermore, that research on education policy does not have to be undertaken at the level of government or state; nor is it necessary to think of such research as large-scale and removed from the immediate context. I try to give examples throughout the book that offer a range of approaches to policy research, from work on global systems to work on individual pupils, and I provide information about the topics that can be researched under the heading of education policy, and about the research resources that are available to students of education policy.

However, as I have already indicated, these elements of the book, which could be understood as forming a conceptual map of the terrain of education policy, do not form its exclusive focus. This is because the book also sets out to try to grapple with some controversial issues that surround research in education policy, and to embed the discussion of research techniques within the larger, framing debate about what research on education policy is, or should be, in whose interests it is undertaken, who does it and how problems in education policy research and resources for addressing them are defined.

It is not difficult to see that 'contested terrain' is an apt description for the field of education policy research. There are no agreed definitions of policy, and researchers who work in this area are of many different types. They pursue the research that they do for different reasons, and may define the most important problems in education policy research in sharply contrasting ways. Not only is there no clear definition of education policy, there are no easily identifiable lines of demarcation between education policy and other areas of social policy. There are many aspects of social policy that raise issues that have implications for education; for example, policy for the family, or for welfare to work.

So there is a continuing debate about how and by whom education policy research should be defined. The main questions in this debate are:

- Is policy research that which is relevant and useful to policy makers (and how do we define useful and relevant, let alone policy makers?).
- Or is policy research properly concerned with critical and independent analysis of education policy making; in other words, with making policy in education the *subject* of scrutiny?

This is a major controversy, and one that places the education policy arena at the centre of current debates about education research more generally – about in whose interests and for what purposes it should be done. That, in turn, is a major question that runs throughout the book, and it generates a further issue to which I give a considerable amount of attention: namely, what do those contrasting positions in relation to policy research imply for the relationship between teachers and research. Are teachers policy researchers, and what does that involve? Are they or should they be pre-occupied with researching and evaluating their own practice, and making use of research evidence for support and guidance? Or do they have a role in scrutinizing policy, and how might that be defended and developed?

For the moment, I want to return to the ways in which education research, particularly education policy research, raises very sharp questions about the definitions, limits and possibilities for teachers of engaging in research. I am going to attempt some coherence in this difficult and contested terrain by taking up an explicit position in relation to these and other questions. I am not seeking uncritical agreement with my arguments; my purpose is to make my position in the general debate clear and explicit, and to leave readers to make their own assessment of its merits. Thus, the book does not try to provide an 'objective' account of all the different points of view on these topics. Instead, it tries to develop an argument about education policy research that is located within the broader debate about education research, and sees education *policy* research as a particularly significant arena or exemplar of these larger debates. Here are my arguments in summary form.

Arguments for policy research in education

- Education research should not be confined to the 'useful' or to research that improves pupil performance. Research should be useful, but usefulness is not a straightforward concept, and enhancing pupil performance, while desirable, is not a sufficient description of the proper and legitimate concerns of education research.
- Teachers should engage in research, where possible and appropriate, in partnership with, and supported by, higher education institutions. All teachers should be encouraged to feel themselves members of a research community, and should be enabled to participate in research debates, and to develop an orientation towards research and enquiry that carries into their professional practice.
- The orientation or disposition to research would serve to foster reflexivity in educational work; that is, a habit of transferring research practices into the education workplace, so that experimentation, scrutiny of results, teamwork, evaluation and the search for improvement in problem solving become natural resources for pedagogic work.
- Research-based practice also creates the obligation of enquiry into the nature of teaching itself, and hence into the purposes of education and the role of the teacher in operationalizing them; this is a legitimate area of enquiry, indeed, a necessary precondition of a healthy profession.
- The capacity to become expert in matters of pedagogy and to pursue reflexivity in matters of professional identity is an obligation on the profession of teaching, at all levels of provision.
- Expertise, together with the acceptance of a social role and the need to negotiate it, confers both status and obligations in relation to the concepts of professionalism and citizenship.
- Education policy research should be available as a resource and as an arena of activity for teachers in all sectors because of its capacity to inform their own policy directions and to encourage autonomous, critical judgement of government policy.
- Education policy research also contributes to the project of fostering citizenship and contributing to 'real democracy' (Dewey 1916).

The book' s engagement with teachers as participants in policy making, and its concern to enhance the capacity for contestation of policy of the profession and the research community generally, follows from taking seriously the consequences of global change. Teachers, in Connell' s words, are:

> strategic participants in the emerging global struggle either to democratise the world system or to maintain it as a structure of inequality. A new order to complexity in educational politics, a new range of possibilities, open up when we consider the meaning of global citizenship and the ways it can be brought into being.

He goes on:

> The way these possibilities are taken up depends to a considerable degree on teachers' capacities for reflection and strategic thinking about their work. If we take seriously the familiar arguments about the growing weight of organised knowledge in modern economies and political systems, then teachers' capacities to operate as designers and producers of knowledge is important to the vitality of education. And, if it is true . . . that school systems have a major though indirect role in social change through the transformation of capacities for practice, then the capacity of teachers to steer that transforming process depends on the growth of their capacity to reflect on their practice.
>
> (Connell 1995: 110)

Research incorporates and sustains reflection on practice. Education policy research requires reflection on the formal construction of practice (and, indeed, of the profession) by policy. It is, therefore, vital to the project of sustaining teachers and educationalists more generally, in order to sustain the larger project of education for democracy. It helps to prevent the reduction of education to conservative or economistic ends. All these points require elaboration.

I am building my argument on to a much larger edifice that has been constructed by those whose project is to understand the broader process of change in which we are embedded, and to maintain critical, independent assessment of them, from a perspective that is concerned about the consequences of new state formations and new accumulation regimes for citizenship and social justice (see, for example, Habermas 1971, 1972, 1974, 1984, 1990; Offe 1985, 1996; Bourdieu 1992, 1993, 1998). One of the strands of their arguments concerns the stripping out of meaning from what were once central concepts in the organization of public life (for example, citizenship, equality, justice – but also, closer to my theme, professionalism), and their replacement with 'hollowed out' concepts like client, consumer, stakeholder, quality, excellence, leadership, performance.

Managerialism is one such 'hollowed out' concept; it is not simply management, but the antidote to public sector professionalism as we knew it. As Clarke and Newman write, it

> has filled the discursive space in which change is conceived. It defines the terrain and direction of change. It expresses the imagined futures and ways of getting there. It establishes the limits of the possible, and imaginable, and, above all, the sayable.
>
> (Clarke and Newman 1997: 52)

So certain things have become literally unspeakable; for example, the defence of 'progressive' educational practice as contributing to the development of collaborative skills and social relationships. The words that we are left with are hollowed out, drained of meaning, or mean the opposite of what they claim to mean (see Readings's (1997) discussion of 'the university of excellence' for a sharp exemplification of this).

Jon Nixon has discussed the elimination of values from the discourse of teaching (Nixon 1995), yet issues of value are needed to challenge technical and rational assumptions about what counts. We are left with a situation in which economy and efficiency are justified *as if they were values*, and other values are deprecated as ideological.

In these processes of change, instability and the hollowing out of meaning, there is a danger of loss of capacity for social practice, especially practice in pursuit of social justice. It becomes more important than ever to sustain 'emancipatory aspirations in a post-modern era' (Kemmis 1994). The current situation is dangerous because the privileging of markets has increased fragmentation, localism and fluctuation, in which 'nearly all factors of social, economic and political life are contingent, elective and gripped by change' (Offe 1996). All this produces steerage and legitimation problems which are 'sorted' by what Habermas calls 'pacification' of the citizen role. As the horizon of choices available becomes larger, so the state becomes more inflexible: 'the state power avenges the damages which threaten it from the side of rights of democratic participation not by abolishing these rights but by developing immunising counter-tendencies that neutralise their actual efficiency and scope' (Offe 1996: 14).

As class antagonism in the old forms dissipates, so citizens become consumers or clients, and their role is 'cleansed of political participation' (Offe 1996). Depoliticization is effected by the invasion of cultural, social and political life by systems of power and money subject to evaluation only within their own truncated terms. This is happening in education policy, and sets limits to the capacity of teachers to claim alternative values and to exploit or develop education's capacity for developing 'real democracy'. Education policy research broadly defined, and in the spirit of contestation that I argue for throughout the book, has the potential to challenge these depoliticizing tendencies, and to help to restore some sense of solidarity.

I return to these issues throughout the book. For the moment I am concerned to make clear that I am arguing the case for a very broad definition of what counts as education policy research, and an equally inclusive and comprehensive position on who should do it, which understands practitioners as policy makers or potential makers of policy, and not just the passive receptacles of policy. I see research on education policy as a valuable resource for the education community, and as a professional obligation and entitlement for educationalists. Thus, my explorations and explanations of education policy research seek to uncover what such research can contribute to the formation and development of independent, informed practitioners, at all levels in the system, with the capacity to scrutinize education policy and to develop their own policy-making skills.

It follows that the materials I introduce and explore are looked at from the point of view of what they contribute to the possibilities for engaged participation in education policy research. They provide ideas for opening up the assumptions of policy makers to questioning, and for making policy research in education accessible as an arena of scrutiny, debate and research for teachers and others working in education, or with an interest in it. I hope that these general points are applicable to a wide variety of contexts, rather than just within the English framework from which most of my examples are drawn. I would also argue that the global issues discussed here bring these issues up the agenda for all educationalists, although the pressures may be less severe in some situations, as differences in policy for teachers within the United Kingdom well demonstrate.

Thus, the coherence of the book's approach comes from the contribution made by the various elements in it to the overall project of making education policy accessible as a focus of research. Two of its main tasks in pursuit of this are:

- To encourage practitioners (and by that term I mean teachers, head-teachers, LEA officers and others involved in the practical work of education, as well as university and college-based researchers and teachers) to engage with policy research in education, so that they are informed about it, and feel that it is accessible to them, and available as a focus of research and enquiry.
- To encourage practitioners to develop a critical and reflexive approach to policy as part of their professional development and responsibility, so that education professionals at whatever level feel not just informed about policy, but capable of independent analysis of it, and of subjecting it to informed criticism. That kind of activity, that sort of critical disposition, would be part of the general orientation of the practitioner towards her task as an educator.

The purposes of education

The statement above is obviously driven by some assumptions about what education should be doing and how it should be done. These assumptions might be subsumed under a label that described my concerns as to do with 'social justice' in education; that is, with the potential that education offers both as a vehicle for improving life chances and opportunities, and as a means of enriching and enhancing the business of living. As we shall see below, such a position does not mean that I assume that all educational activities, organizations and workers in education are benign in their intentions and effects; the fact that I defend these as possibilities does not mean that I am uncritical of present or past provision; nor does it mean that I am blind to the unfair and damaging aspects of that provision. There is, sadly, plenty of research that documents these aspects of education systems, and that illustrates the ways in which they reinforce already existing divisions by rewarding those who have and doing little for those with little. I do believe, however, that education has the potential to go beyond the reproduction of inequality and the maintenance of conservative social formations. Believing in such possibilities is a strong motive force for many people who work in education, and has formed a significant part of the professional identity of educationalists. I would also argue that it has informed much research on policy; as advances in race and gender equality have been assisted by the uncovering of discrimination at all levels of the system by researchers committed to improving equality. Work to reduce barriers to achievement created by inequalities of class has provided impetus for teachers and researchers alike.

What I have arrived at here is a tension at the heart of education, and more particularly at the heart of education policy making, that might briefly be stated as the tension between instrumental policy and education's role as the producer of capacity for social practice (Connell 1995: 97). The idea of 'capacity for social practice' requires some discussion. Connell argues that a major category of educational effects concerns capacities for interaction. These processes operate on the terrain of culture, identity formation and communications. Social interaction, he says, inherently involves creativity; for example, in the use of language. It also involves power, and schools and teachers enable pupils to deal with power, which thus enables the formation of active citizens. This happens because teachers do not simply exert power over students, but develop their capacity through the development of relations based on negotiation, dialogue and cooperation. Current policy seeks to define education as a social institution that produces the capacity to work, 'smartly' if possible, flexibly if not. This one-dimensional view of education refuses to recognize its vital role in the production of social capacity and political practice. Education (as Seddon (1996) argues) is an essential part of the social infrastructure of social life, that which is concerned with enabling, organizing and coordinating social relationships.

That education often operates to reproduce conservative political and social relations illustrates its significance for stability, but does not establish education as only a conservative force.

> The crucial human characteristic involved is not the capacity to learn, which is shared with a range of other species, but the socially-sustained capacity to acquire learning strategies – in a familiar education trade expression – learning how to learn. At the core of education is the creation of a network of workers and practices that sustains this second-order learning capacity both for the individual members and the collectivity.
>
> (Connell 1995: 87–8)

Governments seek to use education for specific purposes: as a means of improving economic productivity, as workforce training, as a sorting and selection mechanism for distributing opportunities. Other purposes have also had some purchase; for example, education has been understood as a site of cultural transmission, as a place where national identities could be fostered – or revised – and as a way of protecting and honouring ideas of heritage that connect to nation and identity.

Within that framework there is a tension between the dominant intention or purpose and the way things work out on the ground, in the schools. Here apparently simple transmission processes become complex, as teachers and pupils modify policy intentions, taking advantage of the spaces between planning and outcomes, as well as the contradictions or competition between purposes. So education, as a policy programme with particular intentions, becomes unstable, because it is always open to renegotiation. In particular, it has been open to broader and more generous definitions of entitlement and to different versions of social capacity from those planned for by government.

Policy for teachers: direct and indirect rule

Those broader definitions have often come from teachers, who have consequently always presented a management problem to government. Thus government is implicated in the management of the teaching profession, and of the education workforce more generally. Teachers have been either managed through the promulgation of a professional ideology, which regulates their behaviour in certain ways, drawing them away from militant unionism and encouraging their co-option into responsible partnership, or regulated directly, through a system of direct specification of curriculum, career structure and professional formation. The cycle of teacher control can be seen as moving through these processes, which we may refer to as *direct* and *indirect* rule. Direct rule has produced disaffection and demoralization in the past, and ultimately a falling off in quality of performance by teachers and pupils. It has also encouraged militancy and alliances with other workers. Indirect rule avoids these pitfalls, but encourages 'licence and insolence' (Lawn 1997) in the occupational group, leads to further expansion of the terms of the 'licence' and is expensive. The system of indirect rule also tends to be associated with liberal approaches to curriculum and pedagogy, rather than utilitarian ones, and thus operates in part against the need to connect the education system to the demands of the economy. So it is expensive, in that it does not deliver appropriate return on investment, and it is expensive because it is inflationary. Teachers want more opportunities for more pupils to participate in more educational activities that are rationed under the system of direct rule; for example, participation in examinations hitherto seen as elite territory, or in music, drama and art.

This is a complex argument, so let me set it out in rather more detail, and explain how it relates to the organization of the book. Teachers feature in the book throughout as an assumed audience (that is, I am assuming that most of the people who read the book will be teachers with an interest in doing policy research), but they are also a principal subject of the book. They feature as the focus of the argument about the need to engage in policy research and research on policy as part of professional responsibility, as a vehicle for enhancing the capacity for educational provision. They are also an interesting policy case; in other words, can we, through the examination of policy *for* teachers, engage more deeply with the debate about the nature of the relationship between teachers and research and policy, by asking questions about what policy for teachers reveals about that relationship?

I would also propose that there are two categories of enquiry to be pursued throughout the book; these are not entirely distinct, but need some separation to assist clarification of the argument. I suggest that the first deals with what policy for teachers tells us about policy makers' views of the appropriate relationship of teachers to research, and the second tells us about teachers as a policy problem or topic. The first encourages the exploration of whether policy for teachers fosters a strong research culture among teachers. What sorts of research (if any) are teachers expected by policy makers to engage in? What resources are available to them? What kind of relationship between research and practice is envisaged by policy makers?

In relation to the second line of enquiry, I am broadening the agenda from the key issue of the teacher–research relationship as envisaged by policy makers into the case of teachers as a focus of policy-making activity, and the questions concern how policy makers have dealt with teachers. What model of the occupational group does policy for teachers contain? What are the tensions between teachers and policy makers, and do these remain constant over time? What do policy makers identify as teachers' main tasks and what resources do they expect to be made available to them? What attitudes and dispositions are intended to be fostered among the occupational group by policies for their professional formation and development?

By looking at the different models of the teaching profession that are currently available, and by looking at the ways in which teachers have modified and adjusted the historical models made available to them by policy makers, I suggest that we can better understand the complex and fluid interrelationship between policy purposes, intentions or planned outcomes, and the interpretation, mediation and enactment of policy 'on the ground', where previous models of the teacher may obstruct the new policy intention. In order to explore these ideas further I want to look at the history of teachers and their relationship with the state, before looking at contemporary models for the profession and their interpretation on the ground by researchers.

This examination of the 'case' of teachers serves as an example of a policy 'problem' – and of attempted solutions – and also exemplifies areas of policy research, while raising issues about interpretation. The first chapter, then, contributes to my main themes about the nature of policy research and of teachers relationship to it, while providing an introduction to one important area of research on policy.

Chapter 2 is concerned with a discussion of the policy case of teachers, using this case to explore research on teachers and what it reveals about policy for them, as well as introducing central questions of interpretation of this policy 'case' that have applicability to all policy research. In Chapter 3, I move on to discuss the interrelationships of theory, values and policy, and ways in which these may be explored. Chapter 4 moves into the policy context, and looks at how research on policy explains and understands that context, and connects it to education. Here, too, I use teachers as a central 'case', but I am also looking at research on the impact of the market principle as a policy mechanism in education. In Chapter 5 I look at resources for research on education policy, starting with the research community itself. Researchers become the focus of enquiry in a discussion of how the policy context has impacted on research and researchers, and how policy for teachers has connected to ideas about appropriate research issues and methodologies. This, of course, forms part of the continuing concern to debate the nature and implications of policy for research in education. The chapter goes on to consider how policy research in education is actually done, and offers a repertoire of methods of enquiry that also connects to the questions of how a policy 'problem' is defined, in whose interests policy research is done and the overall concern of the book to promote independent, reflexive enquiry. Chapter 6 argues for the study of the history of education policy and education policy research in order to understand how research is influenced by prevailing ideologies, and how patterns of educational provision established in the past remain as factors in influencing the shape of current policies.

2 | Teachers as a policy case

Policy stories about teachers

The discussion that follows is informed by research on how policy has shaped, or attempted to shape, the teaching profession in England. Although the material is set in an English context, the themes often have more general applicability. This is my interpretation, drawing on my own work and on the work of people who have developed similar approaches, of themes and events in the history of the teaching profession, and in the contemporary treatment of teachers by policy makers. Teachers are thus presented as a 'case' of policy research, and, at the same time, a variety of research evidence is presented and interpreted. The interpretation follows the logic of my initial position on the desirability of an independent, informed and responsible profession, and, therefore, of policy to realize that aim. Policy makers and researchers with different views of the nature, purpose or potential of education and/or teachers tell a different story.

I argue below that this 'story-telling', through which we make sense of the world, is what researchers do, and is based on a number of connected assumptions about how things ought to be, as well as how things are (and how we know that they are). These assumptions ought to be coherent and consistent, and they also ought to be explicit, so that the reader can see how evidence is being interpreted, through a particular prism. I have made my value position explicit; I shall try to point out, as we work through the 'case', how that affects my interpretation, and I will also offer brief notes on alternative interpretations.

My starting point in this policy story is that the contradictory aims of education, and the different things that it does for state and society, place considerable pressures on teachers and make their work and its management complex and unstable. The history of the teaching profession, perhaps especially in England, is that of a perennial policy problem for which quite different solutions have been attempted at different times, and with varying degrees of success. An understanding of the history of the policy for teachers helps us to see a pattern of relationships between the state and its educational workforce, and it is also the case, in my view, that the historical relationship contributes to how we see and interpret the present. The long-term tension that I believe has existed between teachers and government follows from the nature of teachers' work, and their contradictory and ambivalent role in contributing to the creation of wealth, to legitimating differences in opportunity (while simultaneously challenging them) and to socialization (sometimes in conservative, sometimes in progressive forms, often both at once) (Ozga and Lawn 1981; Connell 1986).

Policy makers are inevitably implicated in the management of the teaching workforce because of the importance of teachers' work in these critical areas, but that management is always problematic, at least in part because policy makers tend to emphasize the economic function of education (though that fluctuates), while teachers align themselves with education as a vehicle for equalizing opportunities and/or enriching experience (though that also fluctuates) (Grace 1985; Lawn 1987; Ozga 1987). The swings in the relationship between state and profession are connected not only to the nature of the tasks that teachers do, but also to the broader context within which they work – in particular to the economic context and the degree of pressure on education to contribute to economic growth, or the degree of pressure on education to build social solidarity or cultural cohesion.

Professionalism as control

The combination of problematic and unstable elements in the relationship between teachers and the state produces swings in the forms of control of the professional group; the essence of my argument is that the teaching workforce is managed *either* through the promulgation of a professional ideology, which regulates behaviour in particular ways (e.g. militant unionism is replaced by responsible co-option) and creates a climate of consultation and curricular autonomy, *or* through direct regulation, which permits curriculum control but provokes militancy and reveals inequity. Neither management strategy is stable: my interpretation of the historical evidence suggests that each strategy contains the seeds of its own destruction. For example, the use of professionalism as a form of control in the late 1960s and 1970s in England encouraged teachers to extend the terms of the professional licence beyond permissible limits, so that there was a movement from grassroots innovation and teacher-led development through to well publicized but relatively rare incidents of 'progressive' pedagogy and direct engagement with political issues (Dale 1981), resulting in revocation of the licence. Conversely, the highly regulated system management of the 1860s led to inefficiency and unacceptable loss of quality (Green 1985).

Teachers thus present a perennial problem within state systems. They are charged with responsibility for delivering particular problem-solving policies, but identify strongly with potentially contradictory agendas that construct education as a positive and public good.

The story below sets out a narrative of the tension between teachers and the state, as understood by researchers (myself included) who see that tension as endemic and the process of its management as broadly cyclical – not because of any 'inevitable' process, but because of the capacity of teachers to pursue agendas that work against the constrictions of direct rule, or that exploit the opportunities of indirect rule. One of the questions that we need to ask, in reviewing current developments, is whether that capacity has been eroded by new, more powerful strategies for the central control of teachers.

From central control to indirect rule and back again

We can start our story by revisiting the period of central control associated with payment by results. In the mid-nineteenth century, we see a turning away from *laissez-faire* and a reliance on private provision and minimal state support for the belated establishment of state education. The establishment of a state system of education in England and Wales required that, along with growing responsibility for the provision of schools, the state assumed growing responsibility for the provision of teachers, for their training and regulation. Before 1862, teachers, who could be certificated, uncertificated or apprentice teachers, were engaged and paid by the managers of the schools in which they taught. With the introduction of the Revised Code, school managers received a single block grant, the amount of which depended partly on the results of examinations carried out by HMI; hence, 'payment by results'.

The Revised Code was intended to be cheap and efficient, but its overarching aim of 'educating our masters' lay behind the narrowness of the curriculum and its rote-learning methods. Before the introduction of the Code, teacher initiatives had raised the quality of working-class education. The Code provided more 'appropriate' education, as Grace explains:

> Despite existing mechanisms of surveillance and screening, the system had perversely developed its own dynamic which had resulted in forms of curriculum development, forms of teacher initiative and forms of cultivation of intelligence which had never been intended for working class schooling. The costs of the enterprise had risen dramatically and new subjects had been introduced into the curriculum. Elementary teachers had become more confident and assertive. As standards within the provided system rose the dreadful prospect that working class education might soon surpass in quality that provided by many middle class private schools suggested, as one writer put it, that there would be an

'inversion in the orders of society'. In short, the system in practice had turned out to be altogether too good for the working class.

(Grace 1985: 7)

The responsibility for this distortion of the schooling system lay with the teachers, who had become, in the eyes of policy makers, an overpaid and overconfident vested interest in education.

Reaction to the code

The operation of the Code provoked resistance from teachers, and was probably the single most significant factor in the development of an organized, unionized teaching force. This, of course, was an unintended consequence of policy. By treating schools as though they were state-owned knowledge factories and teachers as though they were workers, the state revealed to teachers the advantages of organization, and of direct action for the improvement of working conditions. By treating elementary teachers as state servants, the state encouraged them to identify with those whose children they taught, rather than strive unsuccessfully for social promotion.

In the aftermath of the 1914–1918 war, and especially in the post-1920 period, when the bipartite division of educational provision based on social class came under strain, technical justification of such division based on the assessment, through testing, of intellectual ability was invoked. The role of education as a means of maintaining class division grew in importance, as did the need for the state to ensure the cooperation of its teachers. This cooperation could not be relied upon in a period when the NUT had steadily increased its membership and engaged in two long local disputes, while campaigning throughout England and Wales for better working conditions and improved pay. H. A. L. Fisher, the President of the Board of Education, warned that 'an embittered teacher is a social danger' (Grace 1987: 203), and sought ways of reducing that danger.

Licensed professionalism and indirect rule

The strategic response adopted by Fisher centred on policy aimed at encouraging teacher professionalization, within limits. Teachers, including elementary teachers, were to be encouraged to think of themselves as professionals, through the fostering of their responsibilities in certain areas (pedagogic expertise, for example) and identification with the service:

The National Union of Teachers had played a most valuable part in watching over the material interests of the profession . . . but as the state takes a more and more direct interest in the material conditions of the profession, and as these material conditions become more and more improved, then I hope that the activities of the National Union of

Teachers, which is such a powerful instrument for influencing opinion
in this country, may be more and more concentrated upon what I may
call the spiritual and intellectual aspects of the teachers' work.

(Fisher 1919, quoted in Lawn 1987: 69)

Fisher's policy foundered because of the disparity between professional
rhetoric and the worsening economic climate, which led to the implementation of severe cuts in the level of central support for education in 1922.
These cuts, and a review of teachers' salaries, superannuation and pension
rights, aroused fierce opposition from teachers. Teachers continued to swell
the membership of the Labour Party (Lawn 1987), and the NUT was
involved in a protracted salary campaign which involved most of its local
associations in extended disputes or strikes. The Conservative President of
the Board of Education, Eustace Percy, was aware of the danger of overt central control of a politicized teaching force: 'What could be worse . . . than to
encourage a conception that teachers are servants of a government in the
same way as Civil Servants, and therefore must teach in their schools pre-
cisely what any Labour Government may tell them to teach' (Percy, in Lawn
1987: 230). It was this appreciation of the dangers of a highly centralized
system that produced a certain relaxation in curriculum controls over elementary teachers. In 1926, the Board of Education changed the basis of curriculum control from prescription to suggestion, establishing the 'modern
principle of curriculum autonomy' (Grace 1985: 10), which endured until
1988 in England.

My reading of this story suggests that there is a process of policy-making
for the profession here that involved a strategic response by the state to a
number of related problems, including the danger of an over-centralized
system falling into the 'wrong' hands, the drift of some teachers leftwards
and economic difficulties. It is also important in relation to future developments to note that licensed professionalism was underpinned by *curricular*
autonomy.

The strategy of indirect rule continued until 1944, when the political and
social content of expanding demand permitted teachers to defend their
'licensed autonomy' (Dale 1981) and resist more direct rule. They were in
a strong market position in the period following 1944, when there was a
shortage of qualified teachers, public demand for increased educational
opportunity, allied to demands for a more just and egalitarian society,
acceptance of a human capital approach to investment in education and
the growth of pedagogic expertise, whether associated with intelligence
testing or based on child-centred methods. A further important factor was
that which had initially provoked the centre into promulgating licensed
autonomy: the strength of organized teachers (Ozga and Lawn 1988).
Again, it seems important to note that point, and to consider its significance in terms of the way we write and read these policy stories. Here I am

signalling that the mode of control of the teachers, and thus the model of the teacher that policy makers endorsed, was not entirely the product of the policy makers (understood as the system managers and model designers). It was also produced by the actions and understandings of the subjects of that policy, who, by their own actions, set some parameters for the design of the occupation that predominated throughout the 1960s and 1970s.

Throughout the 1950s and 1960s all these factors combined to strengthen teachers' claims to autonomy and to force the state to maintain the rhetoric of indirect rule, partnership and professionalism. It was only with the threat of economic crisis, in the late 1970s, and associated anxiety about social instability that the centre began to move away from indirect rule.

Reasserting control

In England and Wales, the decade leading up to the Education Reform Act (ERA) of 1988 saw intense debate and struggle over education. The debates encompassed a wide variety of topics, and certainly prepared the ground ideologically for the major changes in that Act. That legislation, and in particular attacks on teachers' salaries, conditions of service and negotiating rights, had also generated internal hostility, bitterness, disillusionment and demoralization in the teaching force.

Thus, in England, the ERA represented a key stage in the process of 'modernization', which has gathered pace since Labour came to power in 1997. In the period before the ERA there was a significant shift from straightforward reduction of resource to the more complex agenda of 'revising the ideology' (Dale 1989). Policy documents become preoccupied with standards, and there was official endorsement of the view that they were falling. Progressive educational methods were held responsible for the decline. Progressivism was said to predominate in the English primary classrooms, while secondary schooling standards had been eroded by cross-curricular initiatives which damaged academic subjects and by teachers and teacher educators in pursuit of illegitimate political aims.

The attack on teachers took a particular form in England. It drew its strength not just from concern about economic underperformance but also from anxieties about the subversion of order and authority, the collapse of the conventional family and the apparent growth of alienation and disaffection among youth. Influential commentators suggested that teachers were using the education service as a way of propagating left-wing views, views which were not supportive of existing social structures and which did not support capitalist values. The following quotation from Sir Arnold Weinstock, a prominent and influential industrialist, is a good example of the genre.

Teachers fulfil an essential function in the community, but having themselves chosen not to go into industry, they often deliberately or more
usually unconsciously instil into their pupils a similar bias. In so doing
they are not serving the democratic will. And this is quite apart from the
strong though unquantifiable impression an outsider receives that the
teaching profession has more than its fair share of people who are
actively politically committed to the overthrow of liberal institutions,
democratic will or no democratic will.

(Weinstock 1976: 5–6)

In England, teachers were held responsible for most, if not all, educational ills, but they were held responsible for many other ills as well.
Scapegoating of teaching was a continuous process, from the appearance
of the first *Black Papers* (Cox and Dyson 1969). Teachers have been held
responsible for economic failure, the breakdown of law and order, the
destruction of family life, the erosion of traditional values. Such scapegoating is not a process confined to the tabloid (and 'quality') press, it is
part of the language of policy makers. Seifert (1987) has pointed to the Secretary of State' s provocative handling of the negotiations leading up to
and during the 1986–7 teachers' pay dispute. The settlement of that dispute saw the loss of teachers' negotiating rights and the establishment,
through the Teachers' Pay and Conditions Act 1987, of a teachers' contract. Seifert comments:

The Act gives unprecedented powers to a Secretary of State to impose
pay and conditions on a group of public employees with passing reference only to their employers and unions. It coincides with general policy
over the abolition of national pay bargaining, and the development of
regional and merit payment systems aims at achieving labour market
flexibility while dividing employees against each other. This process has
already begun in mining, the civil service and the national health service. Its main purposes are to circumvent powerful national union
organisations, prepare for private systems, and force down wages
through the competition of worker against worker in regional labour
markets.

(Seifert 1987: 251)

All this was part of the process of reasserting 'direct rule'.
This historically informed interpretation of the ways in which the policy
problem presented by teachers is managed should encourage two responses:
first, the conceptualization of 'teachers' as a policy problem and thus the
development of a critical perspective on policy for teachers; second, a perspective on current policy (including policy for the relationship between
teaching and research) developed in the light of that historical interpretation.

The current state of policy for teachers

There is, of course, considerable difference in the way in which current policy for teachers (in all sectors) is interpreted. There are those who look back to the periods of 'indirect rule' described above and see them as evidence of teacher irresponsibility, politicization and failure to attend to basics. They see the 1990s as a watershed in the transformation of teaching and learning, in which inefficient practices of instruction are finally jettisoned in favour of reliable, proven techniques (Reynolds 1998). Policy for professional formation and career development as pursued by the Teacher Training Agency (TTA) in England is premised on a model of teaching that identifies what works and ensures that teachers use these standardized procedures effectively. The drive for more scientific practice requires a diminishing of the autonomy of the teacher, particularly in making judgements about pupil capacity and the pace and content of learning. This modernizing agenda is pursued within the framework of economic competitiveness as the defining aim of education. Modernization of teaching requires the installation of new production processes (themselves rather old-fashioned in business terms) in the school-as-workplace. The policy makers see schools as clinging to past practices more suited to a cottage industry than to the educational organizations for the new millennium; their technologies are obsolete, their performance is unsatisfactory. The previous policy of the 1980s had relied too heavily on the market as the means of improvement; in the 1990s, and especially under New Labour, we see a shift towards more managed change, through a government providing 'energetic, consistent, imaginative leadership' (Barber 1997). Following business practice, that leadership defines the mission for system and schools as 'world-class education for economic competitiveness', and links improvement to target-setting and monitoring of performance centrally, locally and at school level. Teachers are managed (and changed) through the definition of appropriate prerequisites at different levels of responsibility. These prerequisites began as competences, and have become standards, and they operate both as filters and as performance monitors. In Soucek's (1995) terms, they also encourage an appropriate attitudinal disposition for the modernization project. That disposition is not research-based and capacity forming, and does not contribute to education as a region of social practice.

This, then, is my view of the meaning of current policy for teachers. It is a view that is disputed by other researchers (and by policy makers and those close to them), who see an urgent need to reform the occupational group. Their reasons for this vary, but include the following:

- Teachers are ineffective, and are largely responsible for the failure of the education system. They are failures because they lack adequate expertise and pedagogic skills, and because they dilute what skills they have in pursuing inessential aims that do not contribute to pupil achievement.

- Teachers are ineffective because they have uncritically imbibed sociological theory and research that suggests that education can do very little to make a difference to the life chances of poor pupils, so instead of assisting such pupils to use educational opportunities, they confirm them in their failure by asking very little from them.
- Teachers are failures because they give too little time and attention to competitiveness and success; instead, they focus on social justice concerns (especially race and gender issues) and are preoccupied with the social relations of their pupils, at the expense of their capacity to work, earn and contribute.
- Teachers are failing the system because they have been influenced by higher education, and so promote progressive and anti-establishment/anti-capitalist ideas. In addition, they encourage pupils to question authority and thus subvert the system they are supposed to serve.

These very compressed statements verge on caricature, but convey some of the concerns that combine to make teachers a focus of activity for policy makers. All these shorthand explanations are linked to contestation of the dominant, economizing agenda. They all identify the diverse aims of education as part of the policy problem, and seek a solution through the positioning of the economic as the main, if not the exclusive, educational purpose.

Pressure and support: the New Labour modernization of teachers

The dominance of the economic extends to the policy 'solution' to the problem of teachers. As well as providing teachers with a uniform aim and a homogeneous practice, that policy solution assumes that teachers will be motivated by competition for financial reward. Teachers' performance will be monitored, so that they are under *pressure* to succeed (in competition with one another and with other schools), and they will be offered *support* in the form of financial recognition of achievement; for example, through the Advanced Skills Teacher scheme.

There are differences among commentators and policy advisers or analysts on the redesign or re-engineering of teaching, but all agree that the project has barely begun. Recent policy has been concerned with the restructuring of systems, in particular with the implementation of school self-management. Caldwell (1997) argues that the next stage is the promulgation of the self-managing individual. He quotes approvingly the key elements of job redesign in *The Mosaic of Learning*, David Hargreaves's influential blueprint for school and teacher reform, which proposes that schools of the twenty-first century should:

> have a core of full-time, highly trained professional teachers, on five-year renewable contracts, supported by a range of assistant teachers and part-time teachers who also work in other fields;

contract out substantial parts of their teaching functions, so that secondary pupils spend less of their time in school;

be permeable to their community, to business and the world of working adults, so that the boundaries between school and the outside world weaken.

(Hargreaves 1994: 53–4, quoted in Caldwell 1997: 69)

Caldwell goes on to elaborate on the idea of a highly rewarded, smaller, full-time professional core of teachers, but suggests that much more flexible and imaginative forms of financial arrangement need to be considered by schools, including 'fee for service' payments. He also advocates the use of 'gain-sharing' schemes that reward teachers for the contribution they make to the improved performance of a school. In this scenario, he is anxious to stress that it is the profession as a whole, rather than its management, on which attention should now be focused, and that 'the needs of teachers should move, belatedly, to centre stage' (Caldwell 1997: 71). 'Education of the profession is perhaps the highest priority in the further transformation of school education . . . Teachers should be coaches, counsellors, learning managers, participants, leaders, learners, authors and futurists' (*ibid.*: 71–2). The education provision to sustain these transformations is judged by Caldwell to be desirable through 'an employer contribution to a largely private effort'; this, he argues, will most effectively reskill the profession. He concludes:

> The concept of teaching as *the job* is likely to change, as it will in every field of public and private endeavour, so that a range of professional and para-professional staff will serve the school, some in a more or less permanent core, and an increasing number in contractual, temporary or part-time arrangements. New reward schemes will be required, for traditional career paths and rewards based on advancement in a hierarchy will disappear. Reward in such schemes will be based on performance, including the performance of teams.
>
> The concept of self-management will shift (return) to a focus on the individual . . . While a capacity for personal self-management and the exercise of professional judgement may appear at first sight to be constrained by curriculum and standards frameworks, a comparison with the work of the skilled professional in the medical field suggests unlimited scope in the mission to achieve quality learning for all students. Even the most advanced professionals must work within the protocols and standards that are the hallmarks of their fields.
>
> (*ibid.*: 74)

These proposals indicate the continued strength of the agenda for modernization of the profession, and its likely directions. There are strong indications of increased differentiation within the profession, and of thinking linked to incentives for restructuring teaching careers. In all these discussions, whether they are taking place in New Zealand, or Canada, or England, or Australia, there is a common policy agenda for reliability and standardization of professional practice. In the professional preparation of teachers, for example, the Head of the TTA in England envisages the identification of a repertoire of recognized pedagogic styles from which teachers may select to suit the circumstances (Millet 1998). In an earlier statement, Anthea Millet had set out how she envisaged the TTA tackling what she saw as the fundamental problem of teachers' professionalism:

> My fourth question tonight – which are the essential preconditions for creating a professional framework for teaching? – takes us to the heart of what is currently amiss with teachers and teaching. There is no clear direction, no structure of standards, no framework within which our teachers can progress . . . We must find ways of recognising high quality teachers and rewarding them accordingly.
>
> (Millet 1996)

Lawrie Angus has commented on this tendency of reform policy to assume a homogeneity in recipients of policy, in schools, students and teachers:

> education practice is conceived of in a particularly mechanical way . . . in keeping with economistic definitions of effectiveness, it is the bit that comes between 'input' and 'output'. It is seen largely as a set of techniques, the 'core technology' for managing 'throughput' rather than a complex and always unpredictable process of ongoing construction of educational practice. Practice is imposed rather than constructed, negotiated or asserted; it is a set of techniques to be employed by teacher technicians on malleable pupils.
>
> (Angus 1993: 337)

Similar assumptions can be seen to inform the TTA's new qualification structure for teachers, the National Professional Qualification (NPQ) framework which sets out designated stages in the teaching career: newly qualified teachers (NQTs), expert teachers and subject and school leaders. This, in effect, offers the 'answer' to the question posed by the TTA Chief Executive above. These 'standards' redefine the hierarchy of teaching, and provide very much more closely defined specifications of what the positions within that hierarchy entail. Achievement of these positions is directly linked to training in meeting these specifications, and this has serious implications for the capacity of teachers to design their own work identities. This in turn has implications for what may or may not gain status and recognition as 'professional' work, and for what is permitted in terms of professional work relations.

Underpinning the whole edifice is a set of assumptions about a restricted and homogeneous form of professionalism. Most teachers, according to

Mahony and Hextall (1997), will be defined as technician-professionals: 'working to directives established elsewhere and with little opportunity to engage in negotiation over the parameters and criteria within which they work or the indices which are appropriate for evaluating their practice' (Mahony and Hextall 1997: 8). These policy initiatives purport to offer a sense of direction and purpose to the profession. I want to go on to explore what is lacking from that model of direction and purpose, in order both to continue the examination of teachers as a 'case' of policy research, and to raise the issue of the appropriate role of research in preparing and sustaining the profession of teaching. Before doing that we need to look at the context in which the redesign of teaching is taking place, in order to arrive at a clearer picture of the connections between changing economic circumstances and the redefinition of professionalism.

The economizing of education

Let us explore the idea of education becoming dominated by economic concerns. I am arguing that, in the 1990s, the main function of education is the service of the economy. I would argue further that this emphasis follows from agreement among the nation states of the developed world that they must serve the new, transformed capitalism that has emerged from the crises of the 1970s and now seeks to operate globally through flexible, post-Fordist regimes. Low competitiveness in economies is assumed to be connected to inflexible, old-fashioned forms of education, in the protection of which teachers were heavily implicated. These changes have enormous implications for all 'public' services, and for the design of educational institutions.

The economizing of education has produced the attempted redesign of education systems along less inclusive, more selective lines, with the purpose of reproducing and mirroring the differentiated flexible workforces of the future. These workforces are divided into three tiers, 'highly-skilled, professional and other core workers, specifically-skilled peripheral full-time workers and peripheral part-time or casual workers' (Soucek 1995). Education systems are redesigned to produce these outcomes, and this requires strong interventionist and prescriptive policies from central government, supported by strong managerialist policies at the level of the institution. It also, obviously, requires a definition of teacher professionalism, as accepting of the central control and direction of content and process in education, and of management as responsible for surveillance and monitoring of performance.

Flexibility in the education workforce is secured through the operation of powerful managerial imperatives, and management in this operates as the antidote to bureaucratic professionalism. The system of education is effectively steered through a combination of legislative controls and institutional mechanisms that formally regulate performance, notably inspection and performance indicators. These forms and processes of surveillance extend beyond the formal mechanisms of inspection, assessment and appraisal to encompass assumptions and relationships in teaching. Flexibility can be seen in the changes to initial training that have been in process since the 1980s, which permit different forms of entry to the occupation, and which change the way in which new recruits to teaching are socialized into the profession, especially through specification of content and standards of competence, and through school-based training. Teachers are further stratified through their differential access to professional 'standards' determined by the TTA.

That this is part of a project of restructuring that extends well beyond teaching may be seen by looking at changes in professional work in general. As I indicated earlier, professional work has been a focus of restructuring because of its problematic nature in the modernizing project, and the impact of change may readily be seen in terms of changes in control over pace and process that were previously connected to expertise and knowledge, and in changes in the social relations of the professional workplace.

Professional work and flexibility

Comparisons of public sector professional occupational groups like doctors and the police with teachers (for example, by Bottery 1995) reveal evidence of the effects of restructuring, and close similarities with their effects on teachers. Bottery's study identified the following areas where specific policies had impacted on the professional autonomy of all three groups. They are:

- retrenchment (reduced budgets);
- cost improvement programmes (through tendering);
- renegotiated contracts;
- quality assurance mechanisms;
- appraisal/audit systems;
- diagnosis-related groups (classification of students/patients/functions to allow comparisons);
- performance indicators;
- resource management;
- content control.

These factors were all present and contributing to the diminished autonomy of each of the professional groups. The consequences of these factors for the nature of the work done by each groups are:

- increased responsibility;
- increased paperwork, interfering with the real work;
- increased stress;
- increased entrepreneurialism and control at senior levels;

- little benefit at lower levels;
- increased job insecurity;
- preoccupation with implementing legislation.

These trends describe the consequences of promoting flexibility and restructuring/redesigning professionalism. Some of the consequences of this project may be identified in terms of policy problems as the cycle of direct rule produces its results in low morale, high levels of stress and sickness and problems of recruitment and retention. There may be a falling off in the quality of entrants to the profession; the routinization of teaching, the homogenization of content and the busywork associated with reporting have made teaching unattractive to graduates looking for intellectual challenge, or, indeed, for a chance to do public service.

The picture of the profession overall is not a vibrant one: there is a very poor public image of teaching in England. Nearly two decades of consistent media and political criticism have established a media convention and public perception of inadequacy. Teachers feel undervalued, and are reluctant to encourage their pupils to enter the profession. Recent government responses indicate that the severity of the problem is at least partly recognized. There has been a high-profile recruitment strategy aimed at emphasizing the value of teachers to the nation, along with legislation to introduce a General Teaching Council, and moves to institute performance-related pay, so that very high salaries would be available to 'excellent' teachers (DfEE 1997b).

None of these strategies involves the deconstruction of the model of the practitioner that is implicit – and sometimes explicit – in policy. That practitioner is a 'high reliability' performer, not an artist, a practitioner of moral craft, a guardian of culture or an exemplar of civic responsibility. That practitioner is restricted in the development of capacity for social practice, because of the dominant economizing agenda and because of her own limited capacities for that practice. These capacities are limited because of the narrow and prescriptive approaches of professional formation, because of the social relations that are embedded in the new training programmes and in work practices in education.

Where does research come into this? I would suggest that current policy in relation to teachers and research reinforces the homogenized and restricted model because research is narrowly defined, and offered as a resource to teachers in narrowly defined circumstances. Let us look at this in more detail.

Teachers and research

The summary of policy makers' reasons for teacher failure is quite closely associated with their views of education research and with their distrust of the role of the universities in relation to teachers. Recent policy in England reflects a belief that higher education has contributed to teacher failure in a number of ways; for example, through encouraging teachers to focus on social factors and their apparent consequences, rather than on raising achievement. The place of higher education and research thus becomes a key element in our understanding of the struggle over teacher reformation.

Once again, we can make use of a case study to elucidate this, in this instance the reform of teacher education. The reforms of teacher education – now almost uniformly known as ITT (initial teacher training) – demonstrate a shifting discourse of professional practice from one of service to one of bargaining, as schools and higher education institutions (HEIs) struggle over resources, with the result that there is a loss of trust between schools and universities, a lack of reciprocity, a denial of expertise and an emphasis, as noted above, on decontextualized competence, accompanied by denial of the social context, process and embeddedness of professional work. Distrust of HEIs and the desire to standardize management competences for head-teachers have also led to the TTA takeover of funding and content of in-service provision in education. This has the effect of reducing yet further the opportunities for professionals to engage in the advanced study of education and to do research on topics of their choice.

The move towards reform of ITT and of continuous professional development for serving teachers was part of a more general process of standardization of management of the public sector professionals in order to ensure the more effective operation first of marketization (under the Conservatives) and then of the new public management. The process has gathered momentum, and has led to the current agenda for professional standards. During the playing out of the policy development, the model of the teacher has altered substantially. Even within the reformed paradigm represented by the TTA' s predecessor, the Council for the Accreditation of Teachers (CATE), there was room for a practitioner located in a social context and prepared for complex social conditions. For example, paragraph 6.3 of circular 24/89, which set out criteria for training courses, stipulated that teachers in training should develop an awareness of social background and the ways in which it may impact on pupil attainment, and should be alert to the possible injustice following from gender, class or race stereotyping or discrimination.

That contextualized model implies the need for the preparation of teachers to include understanding of the relationships between social structures and educational outcomes, and their complex interconnections. This implies at least an introduction to some major areas of sociological research, and to some fundamental issues – for example, in connection with race, class and gender and educational attainment – that have been well documented in research terms.

By 1992, the new model for training had become much more focused, and references to an informing context of practice were absent:

Aim of initial teacher training

1.1 All newly-qualified teachers entering maintained schools should
have achieved the levels of knowledge and standards of professional
competence necessary to maintain and improve standards in schools.
(Circular 9/92, para. 1)

The policy document expresses the determination to locate professional formation in a competence-driven mode and to place control of that formation
with the schools and away from the HEIs. This was achieved by specifying
lengthy periods in school for students and by transferring resources from the
higher education sector to the schools to meet their costs in mentoring and
supporting students.

Even with this framework for training in place, pressures for reform continued and led to the establishment of the Teacher Training Agency in 1993,
which was seen to be less susceptible to producer capture than CATE. The
TTA has fostered the development of school-centred initial teacher training
(SCITT) consortia and has manipulated the funding regime to ensure HEI
dependency on meeting its requirements as a precondition of funding.

It is interesting to note, for the purposes of our discussion about research
and teaching, that the TTA signalled early on its determination to capture
control of research funds. It was thwarted, at its inception, by resistance
from the House of Lords, but has made considerable inroads since, and has
now secured standardization of professional development, as outlined
above. It is a very influential contributor to the debate on the future of education research that is in progress as this book is being written. To provide
illumination of that debate, and its implications for policy for teachers and
research, I turn now to two key texts.

These texts were both produced in 1998, but have a significance that
extends well beyond their immediate context. I spend time on them here not
only so that the content of the debate about education research and the place
of teachers in relation to it is elucidated, but also to demonstrate how policy
'steerage' of this debate may influence its content and development. I have
suggested that the message from policy makers about education research and
the role of teachers in relation to it was becoming increasingly clear throughout the 1990s. New Labour's modernized teacher was not depicted as a
researcher, or as working in partnership with HEIs, which were seen, for the
most part, as producers of inappropriate or poor research in education.
Policy makers were able to exploit criticisms of the quality of education
research from a Professor of Education at Cambridge University, David
Hargreaves, who was also a member of the government's Task Force on Standards in Education. Investigation of the accuracy of these criticisms provided
the opportunity for their public endorsement by the Chief Inspector for
Schools, Chris Woodhead. Thus, an apparently neutral process of investigation became part of a policy shift towards greater concentration of

resources for educational research in government-sponsored centres of excellence. The process discussed below also illustrates the degree to which those who purchase research (especially government departments) can design the enquiry. I return to this topic later, and to the issue of reading policy texts like those extracted below with close attention.

Redefining education research: key policy texts

The two texts that I discuss are *Educational Research: A Critique* (Tooley and Darby 1998) and *Excellence in Research in Schools* (Hillage *et al.* 1998). I refer to them as ERAC and ERIS. ERAC was commissioned by the Office for Standards in Education (Ofsted), and carries a foreword by Chris Woodhead, Her Majesty's Chief Inspector for Schools. The ERIS report was commissioned and published by the Department for Education and Employment (DfEE). The reports have related, but not identical, aims. They share a common inspiration in David Hargreaves's 1996 TTA lecture, in which he argued that education research differed from medical research in that it lacked an evidence base to guide practice, and claimed that much of it was 'frankly second-rate educational research that does not make a serious contribution to fundamental theory or knowledge' (Hargreaves 1996: 7). In this lecture, Hargreaves also argued for the establishment of a national forum to direct educational research and ensure its relevance and quality. From that common inspiration, Ofsted and the DfEE constructed two lines of enquiry. One (ERAC) took Hargreaves's criticisms of education research, and used them as a basis for examination of a sample of articles in selected academic journals. The object of the exercise was to test the accuracy of Hargreaves's diagnosis of the problem of educational research.

The ERIS report was less obviously guided in its design by Hargreaves's lecture, and consisted of a review of educational research relating to schools in England. The main aim of the study was:

> to undertake an analysis of the direction, organisation, funding, quality and impact of educational research, primarily in the schools field; and then to pursue recommendations for the development and pursuit of excellence in research relating to schools.
>
> (Hillage *et al.* 1998: ix)

There is no indication of what, if any, relationship there might be between the analysis and the recommendations, but it is made clear, later in the report, that the DfEE expected those recommendations to sustain a set of specific objectives. These were to:

> ensure the relevance and practical value of educational research to teachers, schools, LEAs, Central Government, parents, governors and ultimately pupils;

strengthen the dissemination of good quality research findings to appropriate users and audiences, and the utilisation of those findings;

further the contribution of research to providing a core body of knowledge and related theory;

strengthen the links between research, policy and practice;

promote coherence across the range of research undertaken;

enhance the fitness for purpose, robustness, reliability and validity of research undertaken, and

ensure value for money/quality assurance.

(Hillage *et al.* 1998: 3)

The authors of ERIS go on to say that this list defined the chief task as evaluating the practical value of research in helping to inform the actions and decisions of all those involved in the provision of schooling. The evaluation is thus based on assumptions about the relationship of research to action that assume it to be straightforward, flowing in one direction and practically useful. These are large assumptions. Furthermore, in designing tasks to deliver these objectives, the research team found itself obliged to narrow its range of enquiry:

to meet these requirements, we originally set the following specific objectives for the research:

- to provide an overview of the nature and content of the national educational research programme;
- trace the flows between research, policy and practice, and the ways in which research influences policy and practice;
- assess the quality, value and utility of the output of the educational research programme from the perspectives of research funders, policy makers, researchers and practitioners; and,
- identify ways in which the content of the overall research programme, or elements of the research process, could be improved to the benefit of all the major interested parties.

It became clear . . . that the descriptive elements of what we originally proposed (as expressed in our first two objectives) were less important than the analysis, diagnosis and prescriptive elements of the study (the last two objectives). Therefore, with guidance from the DfEE project managers and the project steering group, we have concentrated on these.

(Hillage *et al.* 1998: 3–4)

Perhaps because Professor Hargreaves was a member of the steering group, the report's authors felt able to assume that an overview of the nature and content of research and a description of its relationship to policy were unnecessary, before proceeding to their more important tasks of analysis, diagnosis and prescription. However, the abandonment of those areas of enquiry does raise questions about the soundness of the report's findings and its prescriptions for action. In relation to the concerns of this book, there are interesting issues about the demands made on contract researchers by powerful policy makers, a topic to which we shall return. For the moment I want to focus on two main issues: first, the way in which research is understood in this report, particularly as displayed in its relationship with teachers; second, the assumptions about connections between research and policy that are embedded in the report.

Research and teachers in ERIS

There is surprisingly little direct discussion of the evidence gathered from teachers in the ERIS report. In all, 23 teachers and headteachers were interviewed, following a schedule (discussion guide) for practitioners that explores their views of critical issues in education, their definitions of best practice and the role of research in assisting them to select 'teaching options' and assess their effectiveness. The responses of practitioners are not analysed or reported directly.

As practitioners are not themselves given a voice in the report, it is necessary, in trying to establish how ERIS sees the teacher–researcher relationship, to try to work out what is implied about that relationship from the research design and from the diagnosis/recommendations. The design reinforces the message that teachers' engagement with research is understood as appropriately confined to useful research on classroom practice. The discussion guide is preoccupied with exploring *relevance*, *effectiveness* and *accessibility*. Only one set of questions recognizes the possibility of teachers as researchers, and there a 'useful outcome' is assumed. There is a preoccupation with dissemination in this discussion guide, and elsewhere in the report. These constructions support an interpretation of the attitude of the researchers to teachers that constructs them as research *recipients*.

While this may be an appropriate element of teachers' relationship to research, in my view it cannot constitute the *only* relationship possible, since it implies that 'research' arrives with teachers in a neat package, with a set of instructions for use. We should also consider what this implies for the ways in which policy makers understand teachers, and what it tells us about the model of the teacher that they imagine and seek to construct.

If the 'problem' with research is that it is not effectively disseminated, then the larger assumption that defines this particular problem is that teachers are deficient in their relationship to research, and this can be 'fixed' by providing guidance on its use. There is an interesting and potentially useful idea here, which, to be fair to ERIS, is treated in some depth in relation to a proposed 'mediation' process between researchers and practitioners, but I think that there are still, from my perspective, worrying indications of a restricted view of teachers and teaching (not to mention research).

Underlying these concerns about a technicist view of teachers in this policy text is a further concern about enhanced central control over professional work. The establishment of a National Forum, endorsed by ERIS, to provide a national strategy for educational research raises concerns about the use of research to support and promote policy. The report lists pragmatic and political objections to such a strategy, including McIntyre's comment that 'a national strategy based on a single set of priorities is as yet unproved' (McIntyre 1998).

The report does not discuss the possibility of research being used to support predetermined policy, but it does say a number of things about the research–policy relationship that imply a very straightforward and technical definition of both policy and research, and their relationship. This can be seen by considering the *Recommendations*:

the strategy behind our proposals is aimed at:

creating more strategic coherence and partnership;

improving the capacity of research to provide support to policy makers and education practitioners, through improving quality;

enhancing the capacity of policy makers and practitioners to receive such support, through improving their involvement in the research process and the development of mediation processes; and

establishing a commitment to evidence-based policy development and approaches to the delivery of education.

(Hillage *et al.* 1998: xii)

It is the last recommendation that reveals an assumption that evidence, if available, will guide policy. This is spelt out in more detail:

Policy makers, at national and local level, should commit to ensuring that wherever possible, policies are developed on the basis of, and/or related to, publicly available research evidence, and encompass clear and independent evaluation strategies.

(Hillage *et al.* 1998: xiv)

Again, this contributes to a particular narrative bringing policy, teachers and research together in a seamless web of enlightened practice, in which research appears to drive the action, without prejudice. This is not a story that refers to my earlier narrative of tension between teachers and policy makers, nor does it allow for circumstances where researchers and/or teachers might have different priorities from those of policy makers.

So the story also makes assumptions about policy makers and policy making in education: that they, and the process, are rational, that there is a 'top-down' flow of energy and ideas that produces planned outcomes and that 'evidence' will produce consensus in practice. Yet the report itself concedes that this is not an accurate picture of policy making in education:

> research is only one of the influences on policy-formation and practice and any impact is likely to be indirect . . . There is no simple model and as a result the impact of research is difficult to isolate and measure . . . given the volume of research, we would have expected a greater level of impact.
>
> (Hillage *et al.* 1998: xi)

And later:

> The routes through which research can exert influence are various. It can act directly on policy makers or practitioners, suggesting, changing or confirming a course of action; cumulatively, through adding to the source of knowledge (Hannon 1998), 'stock of common sense' or 'professional discourse' (Bassey 1998) or *indirectly*, e.g. through assessment instruments, curriculum materials, and pedagogic practices (Hegarty 1998) . . . *Policy and practice are also influenced by other factors, political ideology, pragmatism and personal prejudice among them.*
>
> (Hillage *et al.* 1998: 45–6, emphasis added)

They go on to say that 'this requires policy makers to be more open to assimilating research findings into their decision-making processes than they have been in the past . . . such a commitment can be difficult, especially when research results run counter to ideological aspirations' (pp. 49–50). I revisit the topic of the relationship between policy and research later. For now, I am pointing to the possibility of two competing narratives about teachers, research and policy. In the 'official' version, teachers will become more effective when they are offered clear prescriptions for practice by researchers, within a rational policy framework to which all three groups contribute. In my story, such a passive relationship with research indicates the current, technicist view of teachers, and also reveals a view of policy making that places it very much in control of both research and teaching. This policy text (ERIS) fits into and supports the official version of this policy research–teaching relationship.

The second policy text (ERAC) also contributes to this version, but less directly. My critical reading of it suggests to me that its primary purpose lies in its apparent support for Hargreaves's claim that 'much education research is . . . second rate'. I look at it in detail below when I discuss methodology. Here I look at it as a policy text; that is, as a vehicle or medium for carrying and transmitting a policy message. That message is clearly conveyed in the foreword by Chris Woodhead:

Ofsted inspection evidence confirms what common sense suggests: the better the teaching pupils receive, the more they will learn.

To a significant extent teachers' effectiveness depends, of course, upon their intellectual command of the subject discipline(s) they teach and ultimately their personality. The training they receive as student teachers and teachers in service can, however, have a profound influence on their beliefs about the nature of the educational enterprise and the appropriateness and effectiveness of different teaching methods. The findings of educational research are important because for better or for worse they shape these influences and, in doing so, help to define the intellectual context within which all who are involved in education work.

Ofsted has sponsored this study because we want above all else to help raise standards in the classroom. Eminent academics such as Professor David Hargreaves at Cambridge and Professor Richard Pring at Oxford have expressed their serious concerns about the quality of much educational research that is published today. This study suggests that they are right to be worried. Educational research is not making the contribution it should. Much that is published is, on this analysis, at best no more than an irrelevance and distraction. To justify the expenditure of significant sums of public money, research must both illuminate issues of importance to teachers and exemplify the intellectual integrity upon which the pursuit of excellence ultimately depends (Woodhead in Tooley and Darby 1998: i).

The ERAC authors took the key elements of Hargreaves's 1996 lecture and from them devised criteria for the assessment of a research sample based on journal publications. The criteria were developed around the following themes:

- a serious contribution to fundamental theory or knowledge;
- relevance to practice;
- coordination with preceding/follow-up research.

For the purposes of my present discussion of the relationship between research and teaching as envisaged or delivered in the text, it is useful to look at the extended discussion of the 'relevance to practice' criterion:

Hargreaves' issue of 'relevance to practice' can also be fleshed out in questions reflecting current concerns about the focus of educational research. Here we have interpreted 'practice' broadly to include all of the following:

Is the focus of the research on issues concerned with

- classroom practice?
- increasing educational attainment?
- increasing educational opportunity?

- developing effective school management and organisation?
- education policy related to any of the above?
- developing theoretical perspectives or methodology which move any of the above forward?

But it is not only in the focus of research that the issue of relevance arises, it could also arise in the areas of conduct and presentation. As we have noted above, Hargreaves suggests that the 'gap between researchers and practitioners' is of key concern (Hargreaves 1996, p. 3). By practitioners here, it is assumed we are referring to teachers, head-teachers, advisory teachers, inspectors and similar. The following questions would seem to reflect these concerns in the context of the area of 'relevance to practice', with practitioners defined in the above fashion:

- Is the research conducted by practitioners, or informed by their agendas?
- Is the research presented in such a way as to be accessible to practitioners?'

(Tooley and Darby 1998: 13)

Once again there is, I would suggest, a confluence in the thinking of policy makers and the authors of these policy texts (of course, there may be a case here for arguing that there is a legitimate narrative of improvement and relevance). The wider significance of the largely critical report is indicated in the conclusion by its authors, who suggest that, although education research makes up less than 0.2 per cent of government spending on education (Bassey 1998) it also

> has a wider influence than this figure suggests, for the educational research community is also, by and large, the group currently entrusted with the training and education of future teachers . . . The concerns of educational researchers, then, are likely to be reflected in the culture of teacher education institutions and educational debates more generally, and influence the ethos of schooling for generations to come.
>
> (Tooley and Darby 1998: 73)

The implication is that, as currently practised, educational research is bad for teachers, especially teachers in the process of professional formation.

There are issues about research design that this report raises (and exemplifies), and to which we shall return. For the moment, it is interesting to consider how these research reports, which may claim as research texts the status of supposedly detached and objective assessments of the state of educational research, come to carry so much weight as conveyors of the official line on the proper relationship of research and teachers, and thus of the appropriate relationship of policy to both teachers and research. The detailed scrutiny of the texts offers an exemplification of how such documents may be read and also, to some extent, of how they may be deconstructed; that is, taken apart as policy neutral and reassembled as vehicles for policy. Both texts support the use of policy to set expectations and procedures for research, and design teacher–research relationships within them. Both texts exemplify the use of research to sustain policy.

I have spent a large part of this first chapter setting out my general position on the relationship between education policy research and teachers, in order to explain my orientation towards the task of explicating education policy research. I have also reviewed the current debates about education research and suggested that they form part of an overarching project to reform the education profession, in that the restriction of research capacity and opportunity is a significant blow to the development of engaged, informed professionals. In setting out these arguments, I hope I have also been able to convey the extent to which any discussion of policy research in education is embedded in controversy about the larger framing issues of what education purposes are, and how professionals should best serve them. There is no neutral, Olympian space from which an unbiased, objective account of policy research can be given. We are all partisans but only some of us acknowledge it.

In this chapter, I have presented teachers as a focus of discussion. In particular, I am working towards analysis of the relationships between policy for teachers and the current controversies about education research. I am attempting to use teachers as an exemplification of a policy problem that could well form a topic of education policy research and, at the same time, to set out the basis for my argument that research (and especially policy research) is a fundamental right of and responsibility for teachers.

It is through a historical lens that I would suggest that we understand the fluctuating relationship between teachers and government in England, and elsewhere. The instability of the status of teaching can then be understood not as some peculiarity of the occupational group but as a result of the nature of the enterprise they are engaged in, with all its integral, contradictory demands. At the moment, the direction of policy privileges the economic purposes of education, so that the more social aspects of education are disregarded or denied, since they are seen as a distraction from the central task of raising levels of achievement and hence of economic performance. As the economizing agenda in education has increased in importance, so the other, apparently less productive, aspects of education's purposes are overlooked. Yet education remains in its essence a complex mix of social, political and economic processes. All these processes are important, but there is immense difficulty in maintaining an appropriate balance between all three. In the late 1990s, governments across the globe have placed the emphasis on the economic, and social and political aspects are neglected.

It follows, that teachers become, once again, a focus of policy. Teachers are being reformed in a new mode that makes them less committed to and engaged with the fostering of capacity for social practice beyond the capacities and dispositions needed to labour. In this new version of teacher professionalism, which extends beyond the school into the college and university sectors, there is no scope for the independent, critical practitioner, who has, at the very least, a *connection* to education research that examines policy, including policy for the teaching profession. The new model practitioner is formed through programmes that stress local and practical knowledge, where research capacity is directed only towards raising levels of achievement.

In setting out these arguments I am asserting that teachers' capacity to research or engage with research contributes to their professional identity, and supports the development of interaction with pupils and peers on the terrain of culture and identity. It enhances the ability to develop the capacity for social practice. Furthermore, the possibility of researching education policy contributes to a reflexive project of professional identity that has individual and collective purpose and offers alternatives to 'official knowledge' (Apple 1989).

My argument goes against the grain of current policy in England for the relationship between practitioners and educational research. Clues that this restricted framework may be on offer elsewhere are available across the developed world, where teachers are being subjected to various forms of restructuring. In the late 1990s, the major debates about education research have been on improving its usefulness and relevance for classroom practice that contributes to enhanced pupil performance. The construction of the 'evidence-based professional' as the new model teacher is heavily dependent on a version of educational research that is straightforwardly useful and exclusively directed towards improving performance. Various policy shifts in the funding of education research – for example, in the transfer of funds from the Higher Education Funding Council for England (HEFCE) to the TTA for postgraduate level qualifications in education – have been ways of removing and restricting possibilities for teachers to engage in their own choices of research in education.

Thus, the definition of education research, and of its scope and purposes, is itself a central topic of education policy making, as this book was being written. The direction of the policy shift in education research is directly opposed to the position I argue for in this book. I disagree with the attempt to restrict education research to that which is useful, for reasons that I return to in detail below, but at least in part because without free-ranging research there is no alternative to priorities set by government. In order to consider the relationship between formal policy and research, including questions about what that relationship should be, we need to look at the 'official' over-world of policy, and how it is understood.

3 | Theory, values and policy research in education

In this chapter I look at some different definitions of policy, and review theoretical approaches to policy. My purpose is to develop further the ideas that are implicit in the narrative about teachers, research and policy with which the book opened. In that account, there is a view of policy as something that encompasses all parts of the system, that is not 'fixed' in a specific time, i.e. made and then delivered, and that is contested by all those with an interest in education.

That view of policy has consequences for how research in education policy is done, and what theoretical resources may be drawn upon in doing it. I attempt to explain my argument by looking at a range of approaches to the study of policy (and their associated repertoire of theoretical resources), before considering what kinds of resources are available to researchers working within the critical tradition that I am arguing for in this book. I then consider what kinds of framing of topics of enquiry for the study of education policy-making are suggested by these different approaches, and what sorts of explanations they favour.

Defining policy: projects in the study of education policy

There are many different ways of describing what the study of education policy is, even if we remain within the confines of the 'formal' definition and leave the story of contestation to one side. Terms such as policy analysis, policy science and implementation studies are used interchangeably, or they are contrasted without very clear identification of points of difference. It is not very useful to spend time defining categories, or seeking perfect definitions. However, it may be instructive to ask what the policy 'project' is. Here I am drawing on Roger Dale's use of the term 'project' as meaning intention or purpose, so that differences between these different terms are understood by looking at what the purpose of a piece of policy research is, through asking what the researchers think they are doing and why (Dale 1986: 56).

Through using this approach, and seeking to identify 'domain assumptions' (Gouldner 1971), Dale identifies the following categories of work in policy research: the *social administration* project, the *policy analysis* project and the *social science* project. It is worth noting immediately that these categories were devised before the effects of the turning away from categorical theorizing in the social sciences had really made their mark, so that we should, perhaps, talk about 'a' rather than 'the' social science project, and I will consider the impact of theories of postmodernity on the idea of a 'project'.

Dale attaches the label 'social administration' to the kind of research that dominated education policy from the 1940s to the 1970s, and was also the most substantial presence in the general field of social policy. In this project, the purpose is to use research to change and improve practice, generally administrative practices of the welfare state. The accumulation and testing of core knowledge and the development of fundamental theory take second place to this concern. In Mishra's words, 'social administration is the science of reformism, of administrative intervention and piecemeal social engineering, underpinned by the values of compassion and justice as well as efficiency' (Mishra 1997: 5).

Consequences of this approach include a focus on the national system, as provided by the welfare state, rather than on international, comparative approaches, so that the field becomes rather parochial, together with a preference for 'top-down' interventions in policy, and an emphasis on the collection of empirical data: put crudely, facts rather than theories. Drawing on these points, Taylor-Gooby and Dale comment that a consequence is that 'the welfare state can do nothing more or less than intervene, since capitalism is taken as a given; social administration judges the state's performance within the limits it sets itself' (Taylor-Gooby and Dale 1981: 11). It should be noted, however, that this project seeks to operate at some distance from the official makers of policy; its concerns are focused on the welfare state, however it does not operate in the interests of that state's officials, but in the interests of its clients. Research is carried out in order to improve the client's 'lot', and researchers define the client's need.

If we turn now to the 'policy analysis' project, Dale argues that the primary concern of researchers working in this area is to find ways of ensuring the effective and efficient delivery of social policies 'irrespective of their content'. This may be a rather harsh definition, but it does capture the technicist character of policy analysis, and its preoccupation with outcomes. It seeks solutions to given policy problems. It defines policy as the function and preserve of government: 'Policy analysis is finding out what governments do, why they do it and what difference it makes' (Dye, quoted in Ham and Hill 1993: 4). This is probably as close to a definition as we can get, because as policy analysis has grown in importance throughout the 1970s, 1980s and 1990s, so definitions have proliferated, and the terms policy analysis, policy studies and policy science are used interchangeably. Wildavsky suggests that it is more important to practise policy analysis than to define it (Wildavsky 1979: 410).

This reconnects us to Dale's argument about a 'project' enabling distinctions to be drawn, but unfortunately there is some blurring of the edges around policy analysis, in that it can encompass the academic analysis *of* policy as well as analysis *for* policy. I look at this issue below, in a consideration of the position of the researcher in more detail, but here it is evident that absolute clarity in the use of a term like 'policy analysis' is not guaranteed throughout all the literature that you may encounter in pursuing this as a resource for research in education policy. There is, perhaps, a continuum in this work, from the very direct engagement with policy that Ham and Hill (1993: 6) describe as policy advocacy or salesmanship, to the less action-oriented engagement with understanding policy. However, I agree with Dale that the policy analysis project is more strongly oriented towards finding solutions than enhancing understanding, and there is some debate about how far academics who describe themselves as policy analysts should engage in policy advocacy.

Perhaps the distinctions will become clearer if we move to the final 'project' in Dale's list, the social science project. This he describes as differing from policy analysis in its concern to find out how things work, rather than putting them to work (Dale 1986: 61). Thus, there is a distinction of purpose that is underlined in the difference in 'clients' – the policy analyst seeks to meet clients' needs, to define and clarify their problem, to identify options and assess their effectiveness, the likely obstacles to their implementation and their fitness for purpose. The policy analyst is working within the same framework of action as the policy maker, and is concerned with strategic issues. The social scientist is not oriented towards a client's definition of a problem. The problem is 'defined' by the nature of existing theory, and the orientation is towards improving existing theory; that is, a better understanding of how things work. The orientation is towards the academic discipline, rather than towards the needs of a client or customer, and the rules of the discipline, and its principles of enquiry, guide research practice, rather than a framework of strategic planning requirements and possibilities. Accountability is to the research community, rather than to the customer or sponsor.

Again, there are problems in maintaining watertight distinctions here, as we shall see. And it is perhaps overstating the case to suggest that social scientists are completely disengaged from practice – a great deal depends on the research area. Social scientists working within a social science 'project' may still seek to connect to practice through improving practitioners' understanding of the nature of the problems that they encounter, through better understanding of the social world. Others may seek to influence policy makers as a secondary feature of their work, by adding to the availability of knowledge within the community.

The distinctions have preoccupied me here because they connect to purpose in pursuing policy research, and because they help to make sense of current controversies about the relationship between research and policy (and then between research and teachers). I would argue that the direction and content of policy for teachers suggests the dominance of the policy analysis project rather than the social administration or social science projects. This is hardly surprising – the social administration project was connected to a specific period of policy formation, and rooted in past relationships between governments and academics, in particular as the welfare state was formed and during the first twenty years of its operation. It also connected to the growth of sociology as a discipline in England, particularly to work that was designed to provide concrete evidence about conditions that was offered to policy makers in order to support improvement: the 'political arithmetic' tradition.

The current dominance of the policy analysis project has consequences for how research on policy is defined and for how the relationship between teachers and research is designed by policy makers (following the advice of policy analysts). My discussion of the policy/research texts in Chapter 2 provides support for the contention that policy analysis is becoming the dominant form of research, and also that it is constructing the teacher–research relationship in a restricted and technicist mode.

However, as well as contributing to my narrative about policy, research and teachers, the distinctions between projects help researchers to make informed and self-conscious choices about their orientation to education policy research. My orientation towards a social science 'project' should be apparent from the earlier chapters. You can see how that search for understanding of the relationship between teachers and policy has led to a choice of resources in pursuing that enquiry that has contributed to the narrative of tension that I set out in Chapter 2. The value-orientation of the project is also explicit, and contributes to concerns about the limited view of the relationship of teachers to research that shapes my analysis of these texts.

Chapter 2, then, may be read in part as an argument for a social science 'project' as opposed to the policy analysis 'project' in researching the relationship of teachers, policy and research. At the very least, I would suggest that it is appropriate to recognize that the two projects have different concerns, are directed towards different topics and informed by different values, and draw on different resources.

However, I do not want to give the impression that social science research is inevitably disconnected from practical politics, or that it should be. Academic work on education policy may be of use to teachers, teacher union officials, local government policy makers and education workers at all levels (including those within state bureaucracies). I come back here to the key question of how policy is defined. If policy is understood as the closed preserve of the formal government apparatus of policy making, then it follows that the social science project will make little impact. If, however, we understand policy as involving negotiation, contestation and a struggle between competing groups, as a process rather than an output, then we can see that the social science project may indeed act as a resource. The act of writing this book, the engagement of potential researchers/practitioners with it, may be understood as a contribution to policy – indirectly, of course – that contests the dominant paradigm of policy analysis.

At the heart of these attempts to draw meaningful distinctions between different types of policy research lies the question of values. The values that have been implicit – and sometimes explicit – in my account of policy for teachers have connected to a belief in education as extending social capacity, and the centrality of teachers' role in that. This leads me to view particular kinds of policy for teachers as problematic and to seek ways of sustaining alternative models for the profession. More generally, there is a concern to maintain the capacity of education to contribute to individual and community well-being, beyond the narrow sense of economic contribution.

That value position contributes to the choice of a social science, over a policy analysis, 'project', and also connects to choices about the nature of evidence and its interpretation – in shorthand terms, what we call theory. Let us now spend a little more time on the question of theory and its connection to values.

Theory and its uses

We cannot avoid theory in discussing the nature of research in education policy, particularly if we are working through the idea of 'projects' and asking what sorts of assumptions about the world are embedded in each of the three projects that I have identified. If you remember that the projects in policy research are distinguished from one another by their purposes, then you can see that those purposes will also reflect different values. I need to explore these differences so that you can make more informed choices about your own research purposes and the project with which you wish to be associated.

I want to set out some arguments about the need to *understand* education policy in a theoretically informed way, in order to clarify the rationale for engaging with social science frameworks, and to highlight the importance of theorizing for everyone engaged in education work. In the same way that policy needs to be scrutinized and made more accessible, so too does theory. Theories are useful, indeed essential, to researchers. Research and theorizing are interdependent, and perhaps my approach to theories in education policy research becomes more comprehensible if we understand theories as statements about how things connect, and how things come to happen as they do.

Such a formulation stresses the everyday, routine nature of theorizing. The necessity of theory and its accessibility are more evident if we recognize that we all 'theorize'. If, once again, I revisit the main theme of this book, I might illustrate what I mean by suggesting that we all attempt to make sense of our own situations as workers in education, and the ways in which that situation is constructed, negotiated and/or disputed – in other words, its relationship to policy.

Of course, the level of engagement with theory involved in analysing our own circumstances as an instance of education policy research will vary, depending on the resources available to us and our orientation towards the task; put differently, what sort of project we believe we are engaged in when we do this task. The explanation we reach for in conversation with a colleague may differ from the one we may adopt in completing a formal piece of work on the topic – a master's thesis, for example. In a hurried assessment, without reference to the rules of the discipline, we may seize on explanations that are partial or whose function may be to allocate blame, rather than increase understanding.

So the resources that we draw on, that we call theories, are not all of the same size, weight, complexity or quality. Theories may be quite limited in their scope; for example, they may explain individual cases (a burnt-out colleague, a recalcitrant pupil) or they may point to patterns of phenomena (high wastage rates among experienced teachers, low rates of pay in the 'caring' professions). We need to get to grips with theory, and connect it to the arguments running through this book, because theories help us to sort out our world, and make sense of it. Beyond that, theories provide a guide to action and help to predict what may happen next. We should not, in my view, think about theorizing as though it was an extraordinary or exceptional activity, to be engaged in only in certain conditions, and those to be as far removed as possible from 'normal' life. Nor should we hand over responsibility for theorizing, or for developing perspectives informed by theory, to some specialized group of researchers who are disconnected from educational practice.

This argument about theory should come as no surprise; it is part of the overarching argument about the entitlement and responsibility of those engaged in educational work. It also, self-evidently, contributes to my disagreement with the relationship with research (and by implication theorizing) that is contained in current policy for teachers. It is not so difficult to imagine theory as accessible if we acknowledge that we construct theories routinely. We do this by thinking about information we routinely collect, categorizing it and considering whether or not it may be understood as an instance of some larger pattern. It is, therefore, both inappropriate and impossible to attempt to divorce 'theorizing' from research, or to put them in separate compartments; for example, understanding research as something we do to establish facts that we then make sense of. Rather, the intention is to stress the need to look at what we find out, and what we define as a 'problem' or topic, in a self-conscious, theorized way, while being open and explicit about our theoretical 'hunches'.

Understanding theory in this way underlines the need for explicitness that I advocated above. This is a dynamic and reflexive relationship that prevents us from undertaking research in order to demonstrate the correctness of some static 'grand theory' that dictates the story, but it also prevents research from falling into the contrasting trap of endless accumulation of evidence that tells no story at all.

Of course, the story that is told requires that choices are made. So far in this book there has been a dominant narrative of struggle for teacher autonomy and responsibility in a 'social justice' project, set against the modernizing, economizing project for teachers that seeks to guarantee their efficiency by enhancing their flexibility and encouraging them to accept standardized forms of practice. The two narratives construct very different relationships to research and to theory.

Values in policy research

At this point I return to choice, and to values. In making the choice between possible narratives – and the two offered above are not the only ones available – I turn to values, as these help us to decide which narrative is most convincing and engaging, both as an account of how things are and as a statement of how we want things to be. Researchers are inevitably influenced in their choices about theory by their ideas about how things ought to be. This has been described as an *engaged subjectivity* in the research. As Stanley and Wise put it,

> Our experiences suggest that 'hygienic research' is a reconstructed logic, a mythology which presents an oversimplistic account of research. It is also extremely misleading, in that it emphasises the 'objective' pressure of the researcher and suggest that she can be 'there' without having any greater involvement than simple presence. In contrast, we emphasise that all research involves, as its basis, an interaction, a relationship between researcher and researched.
>
> (Stanley and Wise 1993: 161)

My primary relationship as a researcher is with teachers: as they have been, as they are and as I would like them to be. My ideas about that future state shape how I interpret the past and the present. This illustrates how value positions form the broad background against which theoretical positions are developed or selected, and these in turn impact upon all aspects of research design, including the selection and interpretation of evidence. We need to remind ourselves of differences in purpose among policy researchers; different projects rest on different values and result in different choices of research topic, research relationships and research design. The ways in which values are carried into theory are well set out in Cox's well known elaboration of the differences between problem-solving theory and critical theory:

Theory is always *for* someone and *for* some purpose. All theories have a perspective. Perspectives derive from a position in time and space. The world is seen from a standpoint definable in terms of national or social class, of dominance or subordination, of rising or declining power, of a sense of immobility or of present crisis, of past experience, and of hopes and expectations for the future. Of course, sophisticated theory is never just the expression of a perspective. The more sophisticated a theory is, the more it reflects upon and transcends its own perspective, but the initial perspective is always contained within a theory and is relevant to its explication. There is, accordingly, no such thing as theory in itself, divorced from a standpoint in time and space. When any theory so represents itself, it is the more important to examine it as ideology, and to lay bare its concealed perspective . . .

Theory can serve two distinct purposes. One is a simple, direct response, to be a guide to help solve the problems posed within the terms of the particular perspective which was the point of departure. The other is more reflective upon the process of theorising itself, to become clearly aware of the perspective which gives rise to theorising, and its relation to other perspectives (to achieve a perspective on perspectives), and to open up the possibility of choosing a different valid perspective from which the problematic becomes one of creating an alternative world. Each of these purposes gives rise to a different kind of theory . . .

The first purpose gives rise to *problem-solving theory*. It takes the world as it finds it, with the prevailing social and power relationships and the institutions into which they are organised, as the given framework for action. The general aim of problem-solving is to make these relationships and institutions work smoothly by dealing effectively with particular sources of trouble . . .

The second purpose leads to *critical theory*. It is critical in the sense that it stands apart from the prevailing order of the world and asks how that order came about. Critical theory, unlike problem-solving, does not take institutions and social and power relations for granted but calls them into question by concerning itself with their origins and how and whether they might be in the process of changing. It is directed towards an appraisal of the very framework for action, or problematic, which problem-solving theory accepts as its parameters. Critical theory is directed to the social and political complex as a whole rather than to the separate parts. As a matter of practice, critical theory, like problem solving theory, takes as its starting point some aspect or particular sphere of human activity. But whereas the problem-solving approach leads to further analytical sub-division and limitation of the issue to be dealt with, the critical approach leads towards the construction of a larger picture of the whole of which the initially contemplated part is just one component, and seeks to understand the processes of change in which both parts and whole are involved.

(Cox 1980: 128–30)

Critical theory and social justice

The adoption of critical theory results from a particular value position and resonates with a social science project, though not, perhaps, with pessimistic versions of postmodernism. Its adoption also has certain consequences; it is evident that critical theory in education policy is not implicated in the solution of problems, or at least not in the solution of problems defined exclusively by administrators and policy makers. Working within a critical frame places requirements on the researcher to pursue ethical research principles and to assess research activity in relation to what might be broadly termed social justice concerns (Gewirtz and Ozga 1994). As a result, researchers are placed under an obligation to ask certain questions about the work they intend to do, questions that go back to the core preoccupation with purpose.

Such questions might include consideration of whether the work implies consent to or approval of policies that support the maintenance, justification and legitimization of regulatory institutions that restrict the capacity for autonomous, independent educational development. Other questions might explore whether the planned research offers any potential contribution to freedom from arbitrary, coercive power. Does it support the development of human capacity, respect for human dignity and worth, a more equitable distribution of economic and social goods and an expansion of economic opportunity to meet need? These are all rather abstract and grandiloquent concerns, and might imply that critical theorists have rather inflated expectations of the outcomes of policy research, and of their own significance.

However, I would argue that research can make a contribution to the goals embedded in these questions, particularly if the potential exists for it to be engaged with by the professional community in these terms, rather than in a restricted, technical mode. Research has the potential to contribute in three ways. First, it can draw attention to and challenge the taken for granted or dominant assumptions informing policy; for example, that we must mirror global competition by enhancing competitiveness in our schools. It can also expose the effects of policy on the ground; for example, by highlighting the recent increase in stress among very young pupils following from early testing (Jensen 1998). More generally, it may examine how and where policies increase inequality and impact unfairly on particular groups (for example, pupils with special educational needs who are not selected by schools in competition for market advantage; see Gewirtz 1995). Second, research can set out to explore how injustices and inequalities are produced, reproduced and sustained, in order that we better understand how such processes may be challenged. Third, as Harvey (1990) and Troyna (1994) remind us, research can provide an illumination of injustice and inequity that may assist educationalists in working for change, and helps to challenge 'common-sense' assumptions about the desirability and rationality of the official logic of outcomes and indicators.

This emphasis on critical theory and on using research in the pursuit of social justice connects to my earlier discussion about the responsibility of practitioners to contribute to 'real democracy' and to develop autonomous, independent assessments of policy for education through involvement in research and through the cultivation of a researcherly disposition.

As I argued above, to adopt such a position is to acknowledge that the value position will have a considerable impact on the policy problem chosen for research purposes and on the pursuit of the enquiry itself. Yet it is not only those who clearly and overtly identify their value position and seek to connect it explicitly to a theoretical orientation who are working within a value-laden framework in doing research on education policy – we all are, researchers and policy makers alike. Values are assumptions or beliefs about what is desirable and about how things are. They thus have a powerful impact at the level of pre-theoretical thinking (Dale 1989) or in the formation of subsets of beliefs and assumptions about the world.

As the narratives discussed above suggest, we do not necessarily share these assumptions, either as researchers or as policy makers. Values are contested, they do not have universal currency. Values pervade and infuse our activities as researchers, as they pervade all aspects of social life. I have already argued that they shape our purposes in doing research, but it is necessary also to consider the question of explicitness. By this I mean that values may be so well integrated into our thinking that they shape it in subtle and implicit ways. Their pervasiveness and taken-for-grantedness, along with the assumption in some research traditions that they can be put to one side in the pursuit of objectivity, serve to obscure the differences between analysis and prescription. Some research traditions are quite clear that they are developed from a value position, others seek to be free of such subjectivity, while a considerable amount of research on education does not consider this issue at all, and apparently assumes that there is no connection between theory and values, or that the adoption of particular techniques will ensure objective enquiry.

However, I would argue that our assumptions about how things are or ought to be construct our choices about what it is possible to find out, and about how to find it out. These are our methodological assumptions, and I return to a full discussion of methodology in Chapter 5. Here, I am anxious to emphasize the interrelatedness of values and methodology, so that the case for explicitness about informing assumptions is made still clearer.

Another 'worked example' might help. I have chosen an extract that connects pre-theoretical assumptions and 'gut preferences' to the ways in which different theoretical perspectives on the state are constructed. As well as illuminating my arguments, the extract provides a useful summary of alternative positions on a topic that is of central importance in education policy research, namely the state and what we mean by it. The extract is from Dunleavy and O'Leary's *Theories of the State*, in which they explore the ways in which value positions influence conceptions of the state and its operation:

> There are five components of values relevant to theories of the state:
>
> 1 Views about 'human nature' (also known as 'philosophical anthropologies' lie at the heart of each theory of the state. They crystallise convictions about the basic make-up and driving force of the human character, such as the proposition that 'man is a social animal' or that 'man is born free but everywhere he is in chains'.
> 2 Core moral values indicate how particular theories of the state are related to wider systems of morality.
> 3 Political associations indicate how theories of the state connect up with practical political movements.
> 4 Selections of social phenomena as 'interesting' or 'problematic' indicate how writers in different analytic approaches select aspects of the political process for explicit consideration. Where theories of the state disagree about the importance of being able to explain various phenomena, their disputes often cannot be reconciled by theoretical or empirical arguments.
> 5 'Gut' preferences for particular styles of explanation reflect competing methodological priorities.
>
> (Dunleavy and O'Leary 1987: 337–8)

Dunleavy and O'Leary usefully point up the possibility of incoherence in value positions that underlie theoretical choices. Clear acknowledgement of values – indeed, articulation of them – may assist in developing coherence in the chosen 'project'. Within the social science/critical theory project that I am advocating here, it may mean that when we engage in research activity which takes as its central focus the scrutiny of particular policies and their implementation, there should be a tighter articulation of concerns about the exclusionary, divisive and socially unjust intentions and consequences of such policies, as Power (1993) has argued.

The principle of choice

I want now to focus the discussion on the question of making choices. We have considered choice in policy research in relation to values and their impact on the selection of theoretical resources. I want now to put those together with other factors that contribute to choice, in order to make a case for explicitness in research in policy. In this discussion I shall be drawing on the work of a number of education policy researchers, but particularly on Seddon's (1996) discussion of the principle of choice.

As we shall see in Chapter 5, there is a lot of debate among education policy researchers about how education policy should be understood, and about the best theoretical resources for conceptualizing education policy research. These debates are often about competing interpretations of theoretical positions, and may obscure more than they clarify. However, they are important and helpful in that they add weight to my argument here that researchers on policy should pursue explicitness in their research choices; as Seddon argues, following Howell, choice is inevitable in research, so that if other researchers are to understand fully the principles informing a research project, there must be a commitment to as great a degree of explicitness as possible. Seddon quotes Howell as follows:

> There must be more to policy-oriented research than self-consciously eclectic and wide ranging suggestions. There must be some principle of choice, some justification for drawing the line in one place rather than another. One must have some formulated idea of what to look for, and how and where to look for it.
>
> (Howell 1990: 242)

In considering the implications of that call, and my own discussion of the need to focus on the source, scope and patterning of education policy (Ozga 1990), Seddon identifies a number of contributory factors that make the articulation of the principles of choice in policy research both complex and necessary.

The first issue is the state of theoretical development; that is, the kinds of theoretical resources that are available to students of education policy. We have already seen that there are tensions and divisions among research 'projects' in this field, these tensions broadly reflecting the differences between the competing theoretical paradigms that dominated the area until the early 1990s. The debate encapsulated the differences between policy science or policy analysis and critical social science. The first paradigm was very much informed by pluralistic assumptions; that is, there was an implicit or explicit adherence to the view that policy was made through negotiation and compromise among those who had an interest in it. In education policy this was usually government at local and central levels, organized teachers, parents, pressure groups and business interests. Research in that tradition was generally preoccupied with finding the best solution to a given problem; this is a version of the social administration project discussed earlier.

The second paradigm in policy research, within the critical social science framework, was heavily influenced by Marxist theory, and was thus preoccupied with structural inequality and its reproduction through education policy. The debate, as Seddon points out, and as I indicated above in stressing the diversity of social science and some turning away from 'projects', has moved on. Both pluralism and Marxism have been reworked in response to changing social conditions and changes in social theory, while theories of postmodernity emphasize discontinuities, contingency and the absence of a dominant narrative. A simple polarity of pluralism and Marxism is no longer sufficient to capture the kinds of choices of theoretical resource available to researchers. This is not to say that the 'projects' outlined above are no longer relevant. I believe that they do offer researchers ways of considering their orientation towards a research task.

However, there is now a range of theoretical resources that goes beyond the pluralist/Marxist divide. For example, there has been a considerable recent engagement of feminist thinkers with education policy (for example, Kenway 1994; Mahony 1997; Marshall 1997). Post-structuralist approaches have also challenged the old pluralist/Marxist dichotomy, and elements of these schools of thought have shown signs of convergence (McLennan 1989).

The alterations in the theoretical landscape are important because they have had substantial consequences for researchers. I believe that one consequence of the range of options available has been to produce a tendency towards 'eclectic' use of theory, perhaps because it is so tempting to assume that the broader one's repertoire the more one can explain. At the same time, as the social sciences have themselves turned away from 'categorical' theorizing, there is anxiety about claiming the existence of social life as a totality, let alone explaining it.

Dealing with complexity

Seddon's discussion contextualizes the particular problems of education policy research within this wider framework of change in social theory, thereby making the current diversity and uncertainty of the field more comprehensible. The problem, as she sees it, is not just that of dealing with the revision of hitherto accepted theories, revisions that tend to emphasize the contingent and the fragmented, but that of the possibility of quite new social relations and new experiences of social life, which require new forms of explanation. These explanatory forms seem to me to be most convincing when they bring together structural analyses with sophisticated and detailed understanding of the human agent. A major text that does this is Castells's three volume study, *The Information Age: Economy, Society and Culture*, in which he traces what he calls a condition of structural schizophrenia between function and meaning:

> Political systems are engulfed in a structural crisis of legitimacy, peri-odically wrecked by scandals, essentially dependent on media coverage and personalized leadership, and increasingly isolated from the citi-zenry. Social movements tend to be fragmented, localistic, single-issue oriented, and ephemeral . . . In such a world of uncontrolled, confusing change, people tend to regroup around primary identities: religious, ethnic, territorial, national . . . In a world of global flows of wealth, power, and images, the search for identity, collective or individual, ascribed or constructed, becomes the fundamental source of human meaning . . . Meanwhile, on the other hand, global networks of instru-mental exchanges selectively switch on and off individuals, groups, regions, and even countries, according to their relevance in fulfilling the goals processed in the network, in a relentless flow of strategic decisions.
>
> (Castells 1996: 3)

The tension between policy researchers in their approaches to theory, which can be detected in a number of debates, have resulted in part from the reformation or renewal of social science theorizing in the face of the new situation, as described by Castells, and in the face of its challenge to theory to find ways out of despair and fragmentation that follow from abandon-ment of rational hopes for improvement. Seddon also makes the point that as well as taking account of variety in theoretical resources, we must acknowledge the different ways in which researchers read and interpret the same resource. Her comment below is on the best known debate, that initi-ated by Ball (1993), continued by Henry (1993) and developed in Hatcher and Troyna (1994) and Ball (1994). That debate was largely about how to interpret Marxist theory, in order to achieve a coherent argument in relation to major issues, such as the extent to which the state might be understood as acting in its own interests, or on behalf of capital, which in turn connects to the question of whether policy (of any kind) is best understood as the prod-uct of economic relations. Seddon emphasized the importance of that debate in showing how researchers make different uses of the same theoretical resources:

> the exchanges also demonstrate that common concepts are concep-tualised differently and show that these different understandings are

rooted in the process of intellectual work which generate distinctive interpretations and create a lacework of meaning through the articulation of concepts, assumptions and significations. The debate begins, in other words, to reveal both the intellectual resources on which different policy research is based and the processes of intellectual work involved in appropriating those resources in the formation of a conceptual framework which guides particular policy research.

(Seddon 1996: 199)

Seddon goes on to explain the implications of this recognition of the rootedness of research work, and the processes involved in creating what she calls 'a lacework of meaning'. These are connected to my earlier discussion of seeking to identify research purpose, so that the obligation on the researcher to reveal the principle of choice involves:

an elaboration of the principles which guide our selection of research resources, a clarification of what counts as principled research practice in our appropriation of these resources and in the formation of conceptual frameworks; and the justification of these principles and processes of intellectual work.

(ibid.: 199)

In an earlier publication (Ozga and Gewirtz 1994) which in turn drew on a joint publication with Roger Dale (Dale and Ozga 1989), I tried to identify some of the ways in which it might be possible to make these choices explicit, and I revisit some of the points in that discussion here. First of all, I assumed that it is possible and desirable to seek robust and transferable explanations of education policy, and that these may be at a level of abstraction that enables generalizations and comparisons to be made, but are not so far removed from the detail or substance of any given policy as to have nothing relevant to say about it. I also argued that these explanations should be couched as sustainable propositions that linked education policy to the institutions and discourses of wider society. This involves identifying *what* is to be studied, clarifying the researcher's *orientation* to what is studied and indicating the *perspective* from which the research is undertaken.

Answering the 'what' question produces, for me, a set of necessary characteristics of any education policy that may then be explored in relation to a particular case. That is, I argue that any education policy must have a *source* (or sources), a *scope* and a *pattern*. That is, any education policy has to originate somewhere, it has to contain, however implicitly, some notion of what it is desirable and possible for education systems to achieve, and it has to carry within it some awareness of the workings of the education system and of the potential for change. Going further, I would contend that it is possible to reduce the potential sources of an education policy to three possibilities. That is, I am arguing that education policy can be made only by three major groups within the social formation: the state apparatus itself, the economy and the various institutions of civil society. There is no implication that any one of these groups is always or necessarily dominant in all three dimensions of source, scope and pattern. However, it is argued that the working of the dimensions can always be explained by a particular combination of these groups, and that the particular combination can itself be explained by the economic, political and social conditions and conjunctures of the wider social formation.

I suggest that it is helpful to consider the three possible sources of policy as alternatives, whose predominance shifts. Research could then pay attention to the ways in which global and local conditions, including the current state of politics of education, were framing education policy 'problems', and how the potential policy sources were responding and interacting.

If we then look at the 'how' question, this requires an elaboration of the theoretical framework which shapes the researcher's orientation to what he or she studies. This requires choices; in making these choices we reduce possibilities (it is impossible to keep the 'how' question open indefinitely). The choices we make will depend on the intellectual traditions from which we draw resources, and from our particular use of these resources.

The intention is not to advocate a rigid model, but to suggest that research on education policy adopts certain principles of design that require explicitness in relation to what is being studied, why it is being studied and how. There are many problems with categorizing and interpreting theory, and most researchers 'solve' these problems by drawing on insights from across a range of theories, and by working 'at the margins of theories or in the interstices of them' (Seddon 1996: 200). A condition of genuine exchange in research based on such work is that researchers not only clarify the intellectual traditions within which they are located but also make clear the particular ways in which they are using those traditions. This may involve trying to explain the 'gut feelings' that Dunleavy and O'Leary referred to above, and also demands the unpacking of 'personal baggage' that has been acquired and internalized in the formation of the researcher. As Terri Seddon points out, that 'personal baggage' is constructed both by individual circumstances and by the nature of the field of policy research:

> While the appropriation of intellectual resources by researchers is idiosyncratic, these processes of intellectual work are also shaped by disciplinary formation, prevailing research metaphors and the collective biography of particular research communities.
>
> (Seddon 1996: 201)

As indicated above, there has been some turbulence in the formation of the 'collective biography' of education policy researchers in recent years. Paying attention to that, and to its consequences, emphasizes the distance between this conceptualization of research and positivist assumptions about research. I argued above for acceptance of the researcher's engagement with a research agenda, and against the idea of 'hygienic' research. The emphasis on values and orientation is part of the same argument. Here I am taking further the implications of understanding research (and perhaps particularly research on policy) as a process of knowledge production that is shaped in relationship with changes in society, and reflects them while reflecting on them. Researchers and the resources that they bring to research cannot be ignored as contributory factors in the framing and performance of the research. The research problem is not 'out there' in some world that is external to the researcher; nor, indeed, can we accept the existence of an external world that can be captured and reduced to verifiable fact. Critics of positivism have come from different intellectual traditions to argue against its assumptions and to raise questions about the nature of the relationship between researchers and the empirical world that they investigate, and the knowledge and language that they use as resources.

As a consequence, the issue of choice and explicitness in education policy research becomes ever more complex. In a research culture that was dominated by positivist research, the principle of choice was a 'given', built into the formula of introduction, literature review and methodology. The formula obliged you to provide sufficient information to other researchers so that they could replicate your study, or at least understand how you had arrived at your conclusions and make some judgement on the adequacy of your findings (Seddon 1996: 211). This neat formula has been overturned, but there is no obvious substitute that allows for productive research exchange; what Ball calls 'continuing conversations' (Ball 1994: 174). In my view, that absence (which is understandable, because there is no simple substitute) has left the policy research community, and perhaps the more general education research community, with silences or differences where productive continuing conversations should be. This in turn prevents researchers from extending their conversations with practitioners, and may leave the field open to denigration by policy analysts, who want to deny complexity and restore simplicity.

The influence of the changing context on the production of knowledge also indicates a need to scrutinize major changes in the processes and relationships of policy making in more detail. In England and Wales, as elsewhere in Europe, and in Australia and New Zealand, we have seen the displacement of the old model of welfare state provision. In England and Wales, perhaps to a greater extent than elsewhere, that welfare state was replaced by the operation of the market under the Conservative governments of 1979–97. The process of reformation continues in the modernizing agenda of New Labour. It is interesting to consider how those changes in the appearance of the state have affected researchers' assumptions about how the state ought to act in relation to policy. I am arguing here that changes in the policy context have an impact on how researchers develop ideas about explaining those changes (often at the level of pre-theoretical assumptions), and may influence their choice of 'project' and hence the theoretical resources that they are able to avail themselves of.

In particular, I am concerned here about the tendency of researchers to drift into acceptance of ideologically laden conclusions about the weakening or diminishing of the state in the current context. Policy makers tell us that they have rolled back the state, but we need to be alert to the danger of assuming that the diminishing of state bureaucracy is equivalent to a diminishing of the state itself, rather than its reconfiguration (Rose 1996).

If we examine particular policies, and the cumulative impact of these policies, it is possible to detect a very significant strengthening of state control of education in England, and elsewhere, as others have argued, the small strong state is a powerful force in the regulation of the market, and the dominance of managerialism embeds state influence at the level of the institution and the individual. At this point, it is useful to consider how the context of education policy is understood through policy research.

4 | The context of policy research

New policy formations

As indicated above, this book understands education policy as framed by a process of 'economizing' of education that is common to all developed countries (Kenway 1994) and that shares certain characteristics, particularly in terms of new relationships in the formation of policy, and consequences for institutions and practitioners who are required to accept policy as a guide to action, rather than develop independent judgements. In this chapter, as throughout the book, I am interested in developing an argument about policy, and, in particular, its effects on teachers' capacity and on the capacity of the educational community more generally, including its research capacity. In looking at the policy context and its impact I am following Soucek's arguments about the consequences of the 'new production rules' of public policy formulation (Soucek 1994) through which corporate interests play a strengthened role in policy formation and implementation.

As well as the more obvious 'economizing' consequences discussed above, I am concerned to explore the impact of the less obvious changes; for example, what Grace calls the 'ideological manoeuvre', through which corporate-speak sets the rules for policy discourse in such a way as to privilege corporate interests, while marginalizing others (Grace 1989). Thus, the economizing of education means that economic interests dominate content and process in education, and that in turn requires that what counts as knowledge is redefined, for practitioners as well as pupils. Education becomes the acquisition of the appropriate mix of skills, and a technical consensus is built around concepts such as efficiency, quality and accountability. These are concepts that have been deprived of tension or debate. They are taken to be self-evident, to be self-evidently good, and as 'given' to learners and teachers alike.

Post-Fordist pedagogy

Soucek makes a clear connection between this shift in the educational discourse and the new formations of policy making, to suggest that the push towards formal competencies is connected to a de-democratization of the state (Soucek 1994: 92–3). Soucek argues further that the formal competencies embedded in economized education provision inspire attitudes that fail to take account of the social consequences of their 'rational' approaches to solving social problems. These competencies reflect what he calls a 'post-Fordist pedagogy', which treats the development of moral and social attitudes in the same way as it treats technical and mechanical instruction and learning. In these conditions, learners and teachers are denied the opportunity to develop an orientation towards understanding a given social problem rather than achieving technical success. Soucek sets out some of the consequences for learners as follows:

> Firstly, it does not provide an opportunity for emotional investment in the learning task. Secondly, the student perceives the task as belonging to someone else; the moral dimension implicit in the task is, therefore, unlikely to be internalised by the student. Finally, the student may not perceive it as a 'real' challenge to his or her own capacity to resolve the dilemma creatively and with autonomy. Instead, he or she might see it as an exercise in guessing what the teacher thinks is the 'right' answer.
>
> (Soucek 1994: 97)

The consequences for learners of post-Fordist pedagogy can be extrapolated to consequences for teachers of post-Fordist policy making, as technical pedagogies limit capacity for autonomous judgement, emotional investment and moral purpose. Guessing what the head or inspector wants substitutes for the exploration of alternative solutions that may have social consequences. More widely still, the discourse of policy making for economized education prohibits discussion and dissent. Consensus is achieved only by marginalizing non-hegemonic voices.

> This disposition towards circumscribed discourse then informs the production rules of public policy formulation and directly affects three distinct levels of educational provision: (1) at a public discourse level, it affects what is said about education and who has the right to make claims about it; (2) at a teacher-training level, it determines the course content and the method of intellectual inquiry; and (3) at a classroom level, it predicates the subject matter taught and the type of interaction between students, teachers and administrators. The 'preferred' discourse disposition thus might directly permeate all levels of educational provision from policy formation to classroom delivery.
>
> (Soucek 1994: 90)

Thus, in the area of education policy making, the economizing of education goes well beyond the changes in structures and processes of governance that have been described as market steerage (including devolution of resources) employed by the small, strong state (Ball 1990; Dale 1994), or the redefinition of institutions of governance as part of the attack on 'producer capture' and the redefinition of relationships between state, economy and civil society (Dale 1994). So I am working here with current ideas from the social sciences about globalization and post-Fordism; the arguments in this chapter are foregrounded in ideas and propositions that follow from current thinking about the transition in progress to post-Fordist regimes of accumulation, and the consequences for education systems and processes and those who work in them.

Various elements of policy indicate the economizing of education, including its relocation within the market place, and have replaced its post-war construction as a public good, delivered through the bureaucratic structures of the Keynesian welfare state. It is necessary to understand the two processes of globalization and economizing of education policy, because they have such an impact on potential answers to policy research questions like where education policy comes from, and in whose interests it is made.

Globalization and the economizing agenda are connected, as we have seen. It is the reconfiguration of global capital that requires the redesign of education policy and provision. Globalization reflects economic, cultural and political developments that appear to operate at a level beyond the nation state. It is largely economically driven, but also reflects other changes – for example, in communications, and in the nature of culture – that go beyond the economic. Nation states no longer provide the basic framework of activity and relationships in the economic sphere. Anthony Giddens, like Castells, stresses the impact of new communications technologies and argues that they have transformed our experience and understanding of time and space, so that new networks of communication are established that are not limited by physical proximity or local contexts. For the purposes of the questions that engage us in this text, it is perhaps worth considering the extent to which policy making in education in England is shaped by supranational activity (for example, the impact of the global recession on public sector borrowing may exert stronger pressure on the Labour administration and hence on the shape of provision than specific, internal, education policy making).

There are additional aspects of globalization that link to the economizing of education and connect directly to social science concerns about the impact of these changes on levels of inequality and on the capacity of individuals to develop 'real' democracy. First, there is the removal of policy making from the political sphere and its translation into an abstracted process of rational rule-following, dictated by the need to meet the technical needs of capital. Then there is the extent to which these new networks and flows of resources are unequally distributed both within and across nation states. Globalization is not equally global; new technologies are not uniformly available. Similarly, the impact of these processes is experienced differently within populations. As Soucek suggests, the redesign of education systems requires differentiation in order to meet demand for a differentiated workforce. While some may participate in networks of opportunity that cross barriers of time and space, others will be excluded from participation because of their selection into low-skill, low-security, peripheral employment. So the operation of these processes and their articulation with education system redesign, and new processes of public policy formation, become significant for us as researchers working within the critical policy framework.

In England, a good deal of system redesign has been based on the injection of market principles into the provision of education. This has followed from the dominance of the economic agenda, and the translation of the discourse of neo-liberal economics into a guide to policy making in all spheres of activity, with serious implications for social justice concerns. It will come as no surprise that I argue, following Ball (1994) and others, that the claims that markets are effective vehicles for the improvement of performance and appropriate mechanisms for the appropriate allocation of resource are not borne out by research on the impact of marketization. I look at a specific research study and responses to it below, but I first want to reinforce my constant argument that we must clarify the basis on which we are judging concepts like 'markets' as part of the business of linking up values, theory and research.

There are two opposing value positions embedded in disputes about the impact of markets on education. The first defends the role of the state in ensuring provision through interventionist policies on behalf of its citizens, while acknowledging the limitations and contradictions of such remedial action. The opposing view condemns such intervention as both fruitless and damaging to those on whose behalf the state or the service is acting. There is no meeting point for such opposing views: they depend on very different assumptions about how things are and how they ought to be. An examination of the principles underlying markets will help to explain this.

Market principles

I have stated that the introduction of market principles represented part of the economizing of education. I was referring to the economic philosophy of neo-liberalism; that is, belief in the unfettered free market as economically beneficent allied to political ideas stressing the importance of individual freedom and the need to curtail state intervention and interference in individual lives. These principles have been adopted by ruling political parties across the developed world, despite apparent differences in political complexion. In the UK, but especially in England, marketization has been particularly strong, and remains in place under New Labour, but overlaid with managerialism. The fundamental aims of policy makers who adopt these agendas in education are to remove costs and responsibilities from the state, while simultaneously improving efficiency and individual and institutional responsiveness, and thus raising standards of performance. Education must therefore be stripped of any claims that enable it to be treated differently as a policy arena; instead, it must be understood as more like a commodity, so that parents are encouraged to see provision as a range of products from which they can select.

As with any other form of commodity selling, education is assumed to become more efficient in response to competition. Individual consumers make individual rational economic choices that replace collective political decisions effected through bureaucratic mechanisms. This exercise of choice is understood as morally good, and reflects a rational and realistic view of the nature of society, as summarized in these precepts:

- that individuals know better than the state what is good for them;
- that the market is a more efficient and more just institution for the distribution of goods and services than the welfare state;
- that inequality between individuals and groups is a natural feature of society and cannot be overcome by socially remedial action.

It follows from this set of beliefs that the role of state agencies is nearly always malign and makes things worse rather than better, whatever the stated intentions. As a consequence, policy makers who adhere to these principles attempt to minimize the role of the state to one of support for the operation of the market place and the rectification of the worst excesses of the market.

Markets and social justice

The implications of this agenda are very wide reaching, and extend to the reordering of relationships between state and civil society and the redefinition of those categories. There is a direct connection, in my view, between the processes I discussed above concerning the dominance of a technical, post-Fordist pedagogy, alongside the restriction of capacity for political debate in education, and the apparent reordering of opportunity through rational, natural processes that mirror (theoretical) economic logic. If we maintain our interest in social justice concerns, we have to seek out and scrutinize the processes that ensure that the apparently neutral market works in particular ways, and we also need to ask why this should be so, and in whose interests it is happening.

This requires us to do research into the potential of the market in education in reinforcing inequality, and also, significantly, to engage in research projects that help us to understand how the focus of responsibility for that inequality has been shifted away from the state and on to the unsuccessful consumer and individual pupil, who now bear responsibility (sometimes shared with their teachers) for failure and its consequences in the new post-Fordist, differentiated work order. The success of this policy project depends, then, on the extent to which education policy consumers are persuaded of the logic of the market and its outcomes, even when these are manifestly unfair. How is this done?

Here I borrow Dale's (1994) argument that we need to appreciate that the market has itself been marketed to those who are caught up in it. Once again, the significance of depoliticization of education policy making becomes apparent. The legitimacy of markets is sustained through the process of depoliticization of education. Collective decisions about priorities arrived at through debate, disagreement and the possibility of true consensus are reduced to individual decisions based on the calculation of individual benefit. Ruth Jonathon explains:

> the recourse to market mechanisms to effect the kind of changes in the nature and distribution of education which would be unlikely to secure popular assent if they were introduced through planned policy is one aspect of the changed climate of education policy-making . . . the introduction of market forces should not be seen just as a negative procedure of rolling back the state in order simply to devolve power to the people, with government seeking only to maximise individual freedom. For by delegating to individuals' decisions which, in aggregate, have substantial policy effects, legislators are not lessening the extent to which they direct policy, but covertly changing its direction . . . this procedural change in the policy mechanism brings about substantive changes in the nature and distribution of education, and in the general political economy, and takes such changes out of the proper forum for debate.
>
> (Jonathon 1990: 116–25)

The importance of depoliticization to the project of redesign follows from its role in disguising the polarization of provision said by critics to be implicit in marketization. This polarization follows from middle-class capacity to benefit disproportionately from social policies (Goodwin and Le Grand 1987), and, in education, it reflects the possession of more valuable social and cultural capital. This is not new, as the middle class was able to exploit that capacity to good effect in the days of welfare state provision. However, what markets do is represent social inequality as a natural outcome of individual action in key policy decisions. These are:

• the 'rational' choice that schools inevitably make to select pupils and families with social and cultural capital, which contributes to the virtuous spiral of success, and to reject pupils who may not so contribute;

- the privileging of parental 'exit' rather than 'voice' as a relationship between parents and schools, and the related argument, again advanced by Jonathon in her application of the 'prisoner's dilemma' to education policy, that parents will be obliged to make selfish, competitive decisions in order to gain advantage for their own children at the expense of others and of the community as a whole;
- the privatization of provision, so that individual parents may purchase some services and thus reduce those available to those who cannot pay.

To return to Dale's argument, he maintains that these characteristics produce a multiplier effect that sustains and enhances polarization of provision in ways that differ from the old connection of middle-class advantage and state intervention. Schools thus become vulnerable to the loss of reputation, or to pressure to conform to conservative, traditional modes associated with success. At its worst, this may lead to a mutually reinforcing process of white flight and selective (racist) admission policies. There are further categories of pupil who may find themselves deselected by schools, in a situation of supposed parental choice – special needs pupils, for example (Gewirtz 1995).

Let us now look in detail at a research project that explored the relationship between markets, choice and equity in education, and responses to it.

Controversial research on markets in education

This section considers the research project on parental choice of school conducted by Stephen Ball, Richard Bowe and Sharon Gewirtz between 1991 and 1994 and presented in a range of publications, including the book *Markets, Choice and Equity in Education* (Gewirtz et al. 1995). I concentrate here on the account of the research given in that book.

The research started from the growing evidence that there was a strong association between school choice and social class that worked, as I have already indicated, in favour of middle-class parents (Echols *et al.* 1990; Willms and Echols 1992; David *et al.* 1994; Lauder *et al.* 1994, 1995). The researchers wanted to explore how this actually worked; to seek to establish the nature and complexity of the association and the processes through which it operated to advantage middle-class parents.

The researchers selected settings and samples to provide an appropriate context for their enquiry; that is, one in which competition and choice were significant in the locality. Thus, data collection took place in three local 'clusters' of schools in three LEAs that were chosen to be very different in terms of social class and ethnic mix, and were also contrasted in terms of political control and engagement with the education market. The researchers gathered LEA data on school performance through interviews and documentary sources. The main data collection was through interviews with 137 parents, carried out in three tranches, one for each year of the study. Gewirtz *et al.* explain their procedures for selection of parental interviewees thus:

> The parents were approached through a sample of primary schools which 'feed' the clusters. Respondents were elicited in a number of ways: by letters sent to year 6 class groups; by headteachers at transfer interviews . . . and by direct approach at primary school or at public meetings on transfer. The sample was constructed inductively to match as far as possible the socio-economic and ethnic composition of the three cluster areas, that is, in the third round of interviewing we attempted to target groups which were not well represented in the opportunistic sample gathered in the first two rounds.
>
> (Gewirtz *et al.* 1995: 13)

I return to the issue of sampling below, when I consider criticism of the research design and findings. Here, I want to summarize the claims made by the researchers based on their investigation. These were that

> choice has different meanings in different class and cultural contexts, that it is a socially and culturally constructed phenomenon, and we have illuminated the ways in which families are disadvantaged or privileged as a consequence of the values which inform their conceptions of choice-making . . . In the course of our research we identified three types of parents – the privileged/skilled choosers, the semi-skilled choosers and the disconnected. The privileged/skilled were almost exclusively professional middle class and were inclined to a 'consumerist' approach to school choice. The semi-skilled emanated from a variety of class backgrounds. They were strongly inclined to engage with the market, but did not have the appropriate skills to exploit it to maximise their children's advantage. The disconnected were almost exclusively working class. The market was of limited relevance to them because they were primarily oriented towards their local comprehensive schools.
>
> (Ball and Gewirtz 1997: 575–6)

The book sets out the main findings of the study in more general statements, as follows:

1 The market is a middle-class mode of social engagement,
2 Parental choice of schools is class and 'race' informed,
3 Schools are increasingly oriented towards meeting the perceived demands of middle-class parents,

4 The cumulative effects of findings 1–3 is the 'decomprehensivisation' of secondary schooling.

(Gewirtz *et al.* 1995: 181)

The purpose of the research was to explore the ways in which the relationship between social class and choice operated as a process. The starting point is that there is a strong association between class and choice, as demonstrated in a range of studies (see, for example, Echols *et al.* 1990; Moore and Davenport 1990; Willms and Echols 1992). These studies support the argument that markets do not offer equal opportunities to all to make choices of equivalent value, but instead operate to sustain and, indeed, enlarge already existing differences in the capacity to purchase goods and services. These arguments draw on theoretical resources, as well as on empirical data. These theoretical resources, in turn, derive their orientation from concern about inequality and the tendency of markets to benefit the already privileged.

Gewirtz *et al.* draw on the work of Pierre Bourdieu in *Markets, Choice and Equity*, both as a source for thinking about the operation of advantage and disadvantage in education, and as a guide to exploring the social relations that operate in the process of choice making. I cannot summarize the work of Bourdieu here, but it is important to recognize that he has had an impact on educational sociologists in England since the 1970s, and that much of his work seeks to reveal the processes through which education systems systematically disadvantage working-class children. In particular, his ideas about cultural capital, habitus and symbolic violence provide ideas that challenge the claims made for the market place that I summarized above.

This research has interest for us, then, not only in its design, to which I shall return, but also in the processes that it describes and in the arguments and analysis it offers. It is an example of research that has drawn on critical theory, and that has pursued a particular issue that challenges the truth claims made by advocates of parental choice. It moves beyond the context of the project and its findings in order to subject the claims made by those favouring the market to critical scrutiny.

In mounting that critique, the researchers are concerned to document the consequences of marketization in education for key social justice concerns. They emphasize the likelihood of the class nature of the market being replicated across and beyond England, wherever the form is adopted. They suggest that middle-class parents will always exploit the market to their children's advantage, so that the market perversely allocates goods to children largely in response to their parents' skills and interests (or cultural capital, in Bourdieu's terms). As a consequence of these processes, schools will become increasingly selective and provision will be more sharply segregated by class, so that working-class children, and other children with low market value, will be confined to the least well resourced schools available.

The researchers emphasize that they have explored the processes through which choice actually operates, and that this contradicts the abstract and utopian version of markets that are defended by their proponents. This is an important point, because it connects to the issue of the gap between policy as it is designed, influenced by particular ideologies, and its operation in society. This in turn leads to some very interesting questions about the policy, and how we may understand it. For example:

- Is the apparent discrepancy between market principles and market practice a result of inefficient or inadequate operationalization of market principles? How could we guarantee the 'pure' operation of the market?
- Why do the proponents of markets dismiss or ignore the evidence of connection between class and successful/unsuccessful choice? Is it because they think such differences will wither away as people become more skilled consumers? Or is it because they assume that markets reward deservingness, and (correctly) exclude the needy?
- Is the policy project better understood as economically driven? That is, it permits a better match between investment and outcome than needs-driven policy making. Pupils who represent good investments now get the resources to sustain them, those who don't, don't. So the system is more efficient and more economical, and the hierarchies that emerge in marketized systems reflect fairly accurately the stratified workforces that fast capitalism requires.
- Is a significant part of this policy its ability to do 'symbolic violence'? That is, to guarantee the operation of an inequitable system of distribution of education goods with the complicity of both those who gain most and those who lose.

Such questions connect to what I have termed a social science project rather than to policy analysis. Behind the questions is a concern to find out why things are as they are – in the specific example I have discussed, why do working-class parents choose schools that are more likely to sustain inequality than challenge it? How does disadvantage become operationalized in a system where parents are unanimous in their ambition to do the best for their children? Why do policy makers (perhaps particularly in England) close their eyes to the class-imbued stratification of provision that has reappeared in recent years?

My answers to these questions refer to the changes in social systems and structures with which I started this chapter, to the policy context, and how I understand it and its impact on policy making in education. Of course, there are other versions of the context. One of the strongest critics of the Gewirtz *et al.* book is James Tooley (co-author of ERAC), who challenges the authors of the study on methodological grounds, although it is likely, as we shall see below, that these are a proxy for his disagreement with their view of the market. Tooley maintains that the empirical evidence does not support the case against markets: first, because inequality predates markets; second, because even if there was convincing evidence of increased inequality since marketization this does not prove the case against marketization, it merely signals that we have the wrong kind of market (Tooley 1996: 51–2). 'Authentic' markets, on the other hand,

> would have completely different results. The demand-side mechanisms would bring real market pressure to bear to force up standards – exactly as real market pressure ensures the three supermarkets in my neighbourhood keep up high standards of quality. So, with genuine market mechanisms 'there is a real incentive for schools to vie with one another both in the excellence of their "product" and in the reduction of its cost' . . . and the problem of deteriorating schools might not arise at all.
>
> (Tooley 1996: 53)

The analogy with supermarkets is perhaps unfortunate, as we see increasing concern from health advisers about the emergence of 'food deserts' in areas of the country where supermarket chains are reluctant to offer provision and small shopkeepers charge such high prices that they cannot be used by many local people. These food deserts are, of course, located in areas where there is poor housing, poor transport and high unemployment, and where there are already concerns about the health problems caused by inadequate diet.

Despite Tooley's reservations about it, much of the recent and current research on the impact of marketization supports Ball's argument that inequality is deepening as a consequence of the adoption of market strategies, particularly competition and choice. Not everyone accepts that analysis, as we have seen, and others who are critical of the market have attempted to develop analytical tools that offer versions more compatible with equality of opportunity. For example, Woods and Bagley (1996), following Miller (1989) and Self (1993), suggest that markets should be accepted as a form of system management that is unlikely to be wholly dispensed with by governments, who will not wish to be seen to abolish choice, or reduce devolution of financial control. However they propose that markets in the public services could and should be restructured (as public markets rather than private markets) with different social goals (for example the encouragement of comprehensive schooling). They elaborate as follows:

> It is because the market elements of a public-market are not homogenous or value neutral (Ranson 1988) but socially encapsulated (Etzioni 1988), socially conditioned (Mingione 1991), politically constructed (Ball 1994) and heavily regulated and managed (Levačić 1992) that they can be modified. Above all the need to recognise, debate and make decisions about the values which underpin modes of engagement is an integral part of the notion of the public-market.
>
> (Woods and Bagley 1996: 651)

The authors go on to acknowledge the current dominance of 'free' market principles, especially individualism and self-interest in the current operation of markets in education, but suggest that:

> markets, including those currently operating in education are not characterised solely by competition. They can also contain varying degrees of trust and collaboration (Bradach and Eccles 1991, Granovetter 1992, Levačić and Woods 1994, Hutton 1995). The degree and intensity of internal tensions (between the market and public planning) thus may vary in different forms of public market. Our model would suggest that such tensions are open to ameliorative action, even though they are unlikely to be eliminated.
>
> (Woods and Bagley 1996: 650)

I have included this discussion because it offers a middle way between the acceptance of market principles and the argument that they are not an appropriate form of allocation of public services. Modification of the market to reflect value positions that have been publicly debated and that do not reflect profit or productivist motives offers opportunities for critical engagement to professionals. Research on policy in a marketized context can strengthen that voice by offering evidence of increased injustice and inequity, thereby providing a resource for the profession in reinserting the public element into the market place.

In this chapter we have looked at the ways in which the policy context is framing policy development, and at a critical perspective on the translation of changes in the broader context into educational practices. There has been a focus on marketization, and an attempt to elucidate the ways in which critical social science has understood policy aimed at enhancing parental choice. We have also seen that views of the context and of marketization differ, depending on the value position and hence the orientation of the researcher to the restructuring project. I have tried to show how different positions produce very different forms of enquiry, and suggest different kinds of topics for policy research. I have also tried to explore the ways in which a critical perspective on the influence of the context on policy may assist in the use of resources to contest the hegemonic discourse of choice, efficiency and competition. In the next chapter I look more closely at the issue of resources for critical policy research, and at the impact of the policy context on research on policy.

5 | Resources for policy research

The impact of the policy context on research work in education policy

In this chapter I consider ways of doing policy research in education: what sorts of topics may be investigated, and what kinds of post-positivist methods of investigation are available to policy researchers. This is not a comprehensive review but instead looks at examples of research, especially where attention is paid to the issues of choice that we have already considered, and also where there is a concern with exploring the policy context, not just as a possible factor in policy, but as an element in shaping the choices made in doing research.

This leads me to preface this chapter, which is something of a guide to methodological issues, by first considering the impact of the policy climate – and of specific policies – on the way in which research in education policy is carried out. By that I mean not only how data are gathered and interpreted, but also how the territory is mapped out, how research issues are defined, what the key research problems are seen to be and what ideas are influential in addressing them (and what problems remain unfashionable, and which ideas are set aside). In short, I consider which projects are current in the area of education policy research.

This discussion is a continuation of the earlier discussion of changes in context and related changes in the scope of research that have seen the growth of policy analysis in its problem-solving mode. In the discussion that follows I try to make explicit the relationship between research and policy, so that research may be considered, to a degree at least, as a *product* of policy, in both direct and indirect ways. I also indicate that research concerns and directions are influenced by the prevailing ideological thrust of policy, so that researchers in the post-war period were preoccupied with partnership, and are currently preoccupied with markets and 'steerage' of the system.

An examination of the relationship of policy researchers to the policy context requires some time to be spent looking at the management and funding of research in higher education institutions (HEIs). I have already written about the ways in which changes in the professional training and continuous professional development of teachers have reduced their opportunities for engagement with research, unless it is useful. Here I examine the impact of that context – illustrated in the policy texts that scrutinized education research that we looked at in Chapter 2 – on the research capacity of the major producers of research. This means that we need to look at the impact of managerialism on the research cultures of universities, and of university departments of education (UDEs) in particular.

New management forms and processes in higher education have acted upon previously held assumptions about how research should be done. External measurement of research performance through the Funding Councils' Research Assessment Exercise and competition between institutions for research funding may have had a damaging impact on judgements of quality and worth. The argument is an echo of my concern about the impact of reform on teachers and their work.

My position connects to concern to protect autonomy and diversity in research, and I understand current developments as harmful because I am here drawing on another element in my personal collection of theoretical resources, namely labour process theory, which assumes that work is integral to identity and self-worth, and that freedom to exercise informed judgement in work is a vital part of being human. Changes in policy for research, in my view, have led to changes in the labour process of research that may damage the integrity of the task and diminish the autonomy of the researcher.

Research as labour process

Thinking about research as labour process is not an intellectual resource much drawn upon by education researchers; indeed, there is an assumption, in the small spaces where labour process theory is acknowledged, that it has lost its explanatory purchase in postmodern times. However, there remain powerful arguments, well expressed by Casey (1995), for understanding work and production as primary sites of social analysis and social change, and for using the world of work and associated social relations as a meeting place of social analysis and critical theorizing with the personal and particular understanding of the self, and new formations of identity. We have already seen how this approach can inform research on teachers and their work, and how it contributes to a particular narrative of the damage inflicted on teachers by restructuring and reform processes that deny creativity and usurp trust in the workplace.

I am particularly interested in 'the social relations in which men work' (Marx 1967: 284), in this case when people do research. As in the study of teaching, the social as well as material processes of research production are important, if we are to appreciate the nature of change brought about by current and recent policy. Again, as in the restructuring of teaching and other professional work, I would argue that policy for research has strengthened negative elements in the labour process of research, namely the enactment of hierarchy, division and distinction among researchers, and fragmentation and denial of integrity and creativity in knowledge production. Such a picture of research is all the more powerful because it stands in such sharp contrast to the rhetoric of the research community. That rhetoric claimed that intellectual work offered the integration of the interest of the individual with that of society, without conflict, because in such work the highest capacities of the individual were realized, and fulfilment of the highest interests of the intellectual was taken to serve or complement the general interest. The labour process perspective, in the context of the economizing of education discussed above, alerts us to the significance of the gap between rhetoric and reality. It draws our attention to the composition of the research workforce, for example, and the growth in short-term, insecure contract research work which is done by young men and women (mostly women), with little protection against the expropriation of their labour by established academic workers. It alerts us to the increased steerage of research by government, and to the ways in which responsiveness to policy needs by researchers has been increased through financial mechanisms and through the enhancement of competition, so that independent research is eclipsed by contract compliance.

As well as highlighting the perennial labour process themes of control, hierarchy, fragmentation, economy and resistance in work, we should consider the ways in which a labour process perspective on research draws attention to its transformative potential. Connell (1983), as summarized by Seddon (1996), argues that research is a form of intellectual work in which the intellectual worker, with a specifically developed or underdeveloped capacity to labour, works purposively in a historically specific and socially embedded workplace, with a particular work organization. This labour process involves transforming existing resources, which are the products of earlier work, in the creation of new intellectual products. These products take many forms: books, ideas, articles and frameworks of understanding.

As well as research artefacts, the research process is a significant producer of change. That is, research may bring about further transformation of the researcher, as she or he is altered through the generation of new insights and attitudes. These opportunities for change, which are embedded in research, contribute to its power as an *educational* process, and help to explain why policy makers are so anxious to ensure that research is encountered by teachers only in predictable and limited ways. In Seddon's words, 'the practice of research is also a learning labour process which contributes to the process of subject or self-formation' (Seddon 1996: 202). This insight under-lines the significance of confronting the impact of current material and social processes on self-formation in the research market place, and in the restruc-turing of the relationship between teachers and research, as well as taking account of their consequences for policy research.

We need to return to the issue of context, and in particular to the impact of market forms on research relationships. These may be examined through the perspective that sees them as altering the labour process of research and thus potentially reshaping our identities as researchers. In arguing this, I sug-gest that the policy project of recent years – including policy for education generally and its impact on research, as well as specific policies *for* research – has challenged some fundamental elements of the academic project of research *on* policy, despite the opportunities presented by the increase in activity (there is lots of education policy to research), and despite the appar-ent closeness of some segments of academia to government. In short, there is less opportunity to pursue a social science project in research on education policy, and the version of policy analysis is highly instrumental.

I suggest that changes in funding and in the relationships of control com-bine to deny intrinsic value or integrity to research, especially to policy research, because of the inevitable implication of the researcher in the policy process. As Marginson puts it,

> When economic conceptions of education become applied in education programs, they start to produce the very behaviours that economists of education have imagined. To the extent that university research is com-mercialised, researchers begin to think like entrepreneurs, and the free exchange of knowledge begins to be replaced by the alienation of intel-lectual property.
>
> (Marginson 1993: 19)

I hinted above at some of the ways in which funding and control mechan-isms require a particular kind of disposition or attitude from the researcher, which removes the rule-setting process from the academic discipline itself, and from the critical community of peers. Instead it demands the perform-ance of research production in a particular mode; a mode that in many ways denies the complexity of research both in its processes and in its appli-cations. The researcher is recast as entrepreneur.

The researcher as entrepreneur

The range of factors that have encouraged entrepreneurship is considerable, and their impact powerful, particularly when they are considered cumula-tively. As policy for education is increasingly shaped by changing economic needs, researchers come under pressure to demonstrate the correctness of the assumptions that economic rationalism promulgates. For researchers in education in particular, such a process may require abdication of principles of renewal and improvement through education that had been motivating and informing their research. The dominance of the economic agenda and its assumption of the centrality of competition supports the view that society is intrinsically incoherent and thus entirely dependent on an extrinsic economic logic of coherence (formal exchange through the market) (Pusey 1991: 201). This in turn eliminates rationally driven hopes for improvement, and denies the Habermasian project of discursive redemption in the public sphere, with which intellectuals and professional experts were once aligned, and to which many educationalists subscribed, perhaps naively, perhaps with knowledge of the conservative force of education, but with a commitment to resist it. That project of improvement was once the motive force of intellectual labour, including research, but now new steering mechanisms deliver clear market signals to education, including higher education, and improvement is narrowly defined.

Liberal intellectuals, teachers and researchers remain attracted to the goals of creating 'new communication communities, to give voice to social needs, and to revivify a public sphere that will have "structure-forming effects" on formal processes and structures of organisation' (Pusey 1991: 195). Where such effects persist, they obstruct the operation of the logic of the market, and privilege professional expertise. They interfere with market signals. The market requires a different version of expertise from that traditionally located in the research community, and the new knowledge users (the policy makers) stand in a different, dominant relationship to knowledge production. This differs from a relationship between policy makers and social scientists that involved the latter in subjecting policy to scrutiny in the public interest. As with teachers, professional expertise is an obstacle to reform, and has to be diluted by new relations of production expressed in managerialism. Expertise is undermined by casting doubt on its claims (as in ERAC) and by demanding simplicity, rather than the recognition of complexity.

In such a climate, entrepreneurial research flourishes. There is now much more contract research, which involves not only the handing of a prespecified policy problem to a research team that works within predetermined parameters, but the transformation of the research process itself. For many research workers, the labour is no longer as much concerned with pursuing ideas, collecting data and interpreting them – all the basic propositions of purposeful intellectual enquiry – but with the identification, pursuit and management of research effort. Coordination – of deadlines, contracts, bidding processes – becomes a key skill for core research workers, rather than expertise and understanding of a particular area. Rather than mapping intellectual terrain, researchers now plot the interconnections of networks of fundholders, seek to analyse their intentions and identify their preferred agendas. The constraints on enquiry are very considerable. I would argue that these material and social conditions of research production create compliance with policy objectives and engender high levels of stress among education policy researchers. Again, these are processes that duplicate my reading of the effects of restructuring on teachers, as entrepreneurship is also clearly visible in the more competitive areas of school and college provision.

As in the school system, where the rules of engagement between policy makers and the schools have been shifted constantly, especially where the measurement of performance has been concerned, change is the only constant in research management. The policy agendas of various funding agencies that purchase education research have themselves been vulnerable to fluctuation, so that agency research is characterized by constant shifts, accretions to the specification, amendment and alteration in the presentation. These are very often required from researchers because of pressure on agencies from policy makers. The routinization of these processes and the pace of associated activity ensure that in their transmission researchers become so bound up in the task and in anxiety about its completion that they can no longer work reflexively: as they lose the capacity for full engagement with the enquiry, so they become more intent on listening to the funders, and adept at interpreting even very faint signals from them. The absorption of these signals by researchers parallels, in my view, the absorption of such signals throughout the world of work, and their consequences are particularly marked for public sector professionals, as we have seen.

I would also argue that the social science/critical theory project in education policy research is particularly vulnerable to these pressures. We have looked at the arguments about the impact of the economizing agenda on the processes of policy formation; I am suggesting that those processes carry over into the definition and use of research by policy makers. The mirroring of economistic processes is also to be found in the enhancement of entrepreneurial modes of managing and doing research. These may be attractive to researchers, in the same way that some elements of the same agenda were attractive to headteachers. Successful entrepreneurship, and the marks of distinction it brings with it, act seductively on researchers: the process of bidding and negotiation, the elation of being 'chosen', bring academics closer to power, while the 'just-in time' process of production and adaptation brings the elation of success against the odds, in competition with others, and the stimulation of achievement under pressure. Such competitive forms are now to be found throughout education, and exert a considerable leverage on managers and then, in turn, on teachers and research workers.

As in the school/college context, we should not forget the impact on achieving compliance of powerful external mechanisms of control, notably measures of accountability and performance. Research is now managed at national, institutional and departmental level through a series of interconnected mechanisms that contain a powerful internal logic of competition linked to resources, time and status. As in schools, there are league tables of performance that translate into differential funding and connect to public reputation, which, of course, links directly to recruitment and income earning capacity. As in schools, internal comparisons of departmental performance and internal appraisal systems provide steerage for system managers. In the very insecure world of educational research there is heightened pressure to match the departmental research portfolio to the needs of the policy makers, and to define research problems in their terms.

The addition of that competitive context, and its impact on research work and its social relations, may help to explain some of the divisions in the field of education research generally, but particularly in the area of education policy research. Here there have been recent signs of very vigorous dispute, which may connect to the experience of constraint and possibly enforced collusion in the research community, as it becomes more and more difficult to remain detached from the processes of contract compliance. Then, too, we need to consider the influence of debates in the social sciences, and the threats to the future of some policy work that are posed by the disruption of relationships between teachers and researchers because of changes in formation and professional development and the demand for really useful research from policy makers.

The field as a war zone

Education policy research, despite these difficulties, is an active field. There is considerable debate within it about the currency of different theoretical approaches, and these debates – in their current forms, and in the past – are joined with energy, for they involve values and academic debate is therefore more deeply felt than if only intellectual disagreements were involved. Examples of particularly pointed commentary may be found in Ball (1993), Henry (1993), Power (1993), Hatcher and Troyna (1994). My intention here is not to consider the content of the debate, but to note its existence and its nature. It is interesting to speculate on the reasons for the hostile and, indeed, personal terms in which it is conducted. There is certainly a need for energetic debate about the field, but it is puzzling that it has taken this particular unproductive character. Perhaps this is partly a consequence of the changes discussed above, perhaps it follows from frustration and disappointment as policy analysis, in a narrow form, triumphed.

The history of education policy research was connected to the social administration 'project' and to theory that sustained 'rationally driven hopes for improvement'. The apparent failure of that enlightenment project has left educational research without a strong, independent claim to influence on policy. In the post-war period of human capital theory and liberal democratic assumptions about equality of opportunity, social research on education had a strong policy orientation. It also influenced policy in the post-war political arithmetic tradition, embodied in Halsey's work and the explicit commitment to the collection of objective facts about the social world and their use as a basis for social reform through government's informed action to create a more just society. The 1960s saw a high point of academic influence on policy; education was the main focus of social engineering, and academics were instrumental in the shaping of Labour Party policy in opposition and in power.

There was a utopian view of the possibilities of education and a linear, rational view of policy making. The social reform project failed, and the new sociology of education carried within it, along with a commitment to social change, a degree of pessimism about its possibility through education. In Dale's analysis, their iconoclastic role as critics of utopianism left sociologists with a pyrrhic victory and created the conditions in which the 1997 Greenwich lecturer could describe the contribution of the sociology of education as 'the equivalent of saying that the poor are always with us' (Barber 1997).

A further factor contributing to the unsatisfactory and disputatious engagement with theory in education policy research follows perhaps from the rather disconnected relationship of education policy research to developments in social science thinking, and from the general field of changing social policy, so that, with some exceptions, there is little use of concepts and theories that have been applied in these fields. Where take-up exists, it is often at the level of what Dale (1992) calls 'theory by numbers', and what Ball describes as 'mantric, and simply gesturally featured: a process of concept matching, the search for a case of governmentality, patriarchy, state oppression, post-Fordism. Theory as finger pointing (Ball 1997: 269).

The reduction of theory to slogans is possibly a factor in the absence of a healthy and reflexive exchange between policy researchers, comparable to that in other areas of social policy. Indeed, Stephen Ball suggests that it was the actions of policy makers, particularly in the Education Act 1988 in England, that revived the study of education policy, rather than any development in academic debate (Ball 1994). He considers that the plethora of studies of policy since 1988 has brought little in the way of conceptual advance or advances in the theorization of policy. I made a similar point in raising concerns about the direction of education policy studies following a mapping of their proposed research terrain in relation to the grant maintained schools policy by David Halpin and John Fitz (1990). That programme seemed to me to be preoccupied with providing detailed descriptions of elements of a specific policy, but neglected attempts at explanation or synthesis (Ozga 1990).

There is, in the current state of education policy research, I would argue, evidence that these concerns have been borne out in practice, and that the field has been preoccupied with internal disputes about interpretation of theoretical resources on the one hand, and detailed description of how policies work on the other. In addition, because of the changes in the production processes of research referred to above, policy research is driven by the policy makers, and is thus preoccupied with implementation studies, rather than with asking fundamental questions about the nature of policy.

Theoretical developments combined with shifts in policy making to put some pressure on education policy researchers. This pressure is financial and intellectual, externally generated and internally mediated and absorbed. The issue of changing theoretical resources has already been discussed, but perhaps should be seen in relation to the disputed context of the field of education policy studies. Education policy researchers were faced with the need to explore more explicitly the consequences for education policy research of shifting from 'categorical' analysis (Connell 1987) towards understanding individual and collective action through its institutional and discursive framing and shaping, a movement described by Law (1995) as that from a theory of nouns to a theory of verbs. That theory of verbs insisted that policy researchers encountered participants in education as active, knowing agents. Those agents may have incomplete or inadequate knowledge, and their ability to act may be circumscribed, but it was an essential part of the theoretical turn that they were understood as simultaneously absorbing and refashioning institutional/cultural expectations within the context of education. In addition, elements of the postmodern turn challenged the project of rationally driven hopes for improvement. As we have already seen, these theoretical shifts were demanding of researchers, and may help to explain the energy with which internal disputes have been joined.

Policy-controlled and self-controlled research

In putting all these ingredients together in order to arrive at an assessment of the current state of the field, it may be useful to attempt, once more, to clarify research purposes. Here I shall draw on Simon Marginson's (1993) attempt to distinguish between policy-controlled and self-controlled research, also discussed by Moore (1996). Marginson stresses that although there is a difference between policy-controlled and self-controlled research, it is not one of quality, nor of breadth. Both types could and should be rigorous and scholarly. There is no straightforward polarity of academic autonomy and state instrumentalism, as no research is separate from policy. Rather, the difference lies in the contrasting forms of relationship between knowledge and power in the practice of research. Knowledge and power are interpenetrated and the point at issue is the balance of power. Policy-controlled research is governed by the pre-given needs and language of policy makers; self-controlled research permits researchers to define their own agendas and their own relationship to policy.

Self-controlled research, Marginson argues, is not necessarily less norma-tive; the difference is that the norms are established by the researchers, not by policy makers. So there is a certain indeterminacy between this research and policy: not separation, because producers of knowledge are producers of power relations. Universities, he writes, are thus never innocent of relations of power. The strategic development of a field of knowledge, he argues, has the potential to shape the environment in which policy is con-ducted (including public and expert opinion) and even directly to influence policy.

Policy-controlled research uses the assumptions and modes of communi-cation of policy makers. In Marginson's words:

> In policy controlled research there is a tendency to adopt the assump-tions and modes of communication of the policy-makers, because the effectiveness of this mode of research depends on a high degree of inte-gration with the processes of policy development and implementation. As policy actors, the researchers become more effective if they are able to use the same language as government officials and politicians, and perhaps also journalists and representatives of interest groups.
>
> (Marginson 1993: 17)

Policy-controlled research, according to Marginson, has symbolic, constitu-tive and investigative roles. Research which is confined to the elaboration of a pre-given policy may still be research, provided that it has created new knowledge in the process. Where there is no reciprocity between research and policy, when the research fails to create new knowledge, and becomes identical to policy, then we are talking not about research but about propa-ganda (Marginson 1993: 18).

In exploring further the relationship between self-controlled research and policy, Marginson argues that it is only through rare coincidence of interest that self-controlled research has an instrumental role in policy. But it does have conceptual forms of influence, in that it builds long-term, internally coherent programmes designed to influence the discursive frameworks within which policy is formed. Work to facilitate this influence should be done by the academic community with the wider public, he argues. Funding pressures on self-controlled research could be eased, he suggests, by a process of internal taxation of policy-controlled research to support inde-pendent investigation, so that those who are successful in winning sponsor-ship from policy makers should be tithed to ensure the continuation of independent research.

He makes two further points: first, that education policy needs an interdisciplinary framework for study; second, that there is very consider-able scope for self-controlled research in education policy. The need for an interdisciplinary framework has already been argued throughout this book; it refers essentially to ensuring that education policy research happens within a social science project and is not confined to narrow disciplinary parameters that do not take account of influences on education policy from the wider world. On the second point, Marginson proposes interesting examples that contribute to a reflexive agenda that studies the material conditions of academic labour and the politics of knowledge production. He suggests, in fact, that researchers study themselves, and that work in policy research on higher education should include critical histories, studies of institutional forms and academic freedom and research into the relationship between HEIs and government. He also proposes comparative studies of academic cultures, research on higher education and professional formation and research on research production and the conditions that govern it.

Marginson concludes his discussion with some concrete examples of the need for self-controlled research that incorporates an independent and critical approach. He selects cases that concern the relationship between research-based knowledge and areas of policy making that are sensitive. He argues that:

> In each case, research (or hypothetical research) was used as the basis for claims that government spending on education was ineffective and therefore dispensable. In each case the independent research communities have been largely silent and the official policy interpretation of the research has become dominant.
>
> (Marginson 1993: 24)

The first example concerns *class sizes and educational attainment*. The education policy literature has largely concluded that there is no relationship between smaller class sizes and improved educational attainment as measured in standardized tests of achievement. Most of this research is American. Marginson cites the study by Glass and Smith (1979), which consisted of a meta-analysis of studies of the relationship between class size and educational achievement. That analysis indicated that in the normal class size range of 15–40 students, there was not much variation in achievement levels. Marginson then traces the influence of that article as it entered the economics of education, where Hanushek (1986: 1148) used it to infer that 'the constantly rising costs and quantity of the inputs appear unmatched by improvement in the performance of students.' He then suggests that it was influential with policy makers because it supported their aims of reducing public spending. Alternative arguments – for example, pointing out that standardized testing made a difference to the findings, and that larger numbers would have eliminated other rewarding classroom activities – have been dismissed as special pleading by the teacher associations.

Marginson's second case concerns *public choice theory and education spending*. Here he is illustrating the effects of ideological commitment by policy makers on their interpretation of evidence and their subsequent action. The study he examines was carried out by the Institute of Public

Affairs (IPA) and consisted of a survey of costs in public sector provision in the different states of Australia. The policy recommendation, subsequently accepted by policy makers and repeated in the media, was to cut spending in state systems with higher than national average expenditure. This policy was a direct reflection of the strength of public choice theory, which dictated the way in which this evidence was interpreted, as follows:

> Drawing on public choice theory, we have started from the assumption that, unless there is evidence to the contrary, high staffing ratios do not provide a better quality service and are a reflection of other factors, such as vote 'buying' of public sector unions and other similar pressure groups, or attempts to minimise potential vote losses from similar groups by politicians . . . The higher levels of spending in such states as Victoria and Tasmania appear to have more to do with the 'capture' of governments in those states by teachers' unions, than with a genuine policy to lift educational standards . . . Accordingly, there seems to be large savings to be made (without any necessary diminution of educational quality).
>
> (IPA, quoted in Marginson 1993)

The dominance of public choice theory made it impossible to present those higher levels of spending as improved public goods for the students in those states.

The third example cited by Marginson concerns events leading up to the introduction of *fees in higher education in Australia*. The introduction of the Higher Education Contribution Scheme (HECS) in 1988, was made easier for policy makers, he argues, because of claims that the abolition of fees in 1974 had not led to a more egalitarian social mix in the student body. Policy makers and their advisers were able to make these claims because no long-term, longitudinal research programme on student background existed; there were only snapshots of different institutional data, from which a particular interpretation was drawn. In fact, Marginson argues that there were data that allowed for a case to be made that higher education in Australia had become more representative of the total population since the abolition of fees, in particular through the greater presence of women. But these arguments were not made, and the public perception of the policy change was that it would make little difference. This enabled the introduction of HECS, which are essentially loan schemes through which graduates repay the costs of their higher education. The rates of repayment have recently been increased, but researchers concerned about the impact on access have been unable to make this case successfully to policy makers.

These examples from the Australian context not only illuminate the ways in which research for policy produces the answers that policy makers expect to hear, but also illustrate how alternative interpretations of relevant evidence are dismissed or denied. There are plenty of examples of this kind of policy–research relationship. My point is not so much to demonstrate their existence but to look at their consequences for independent research; the power they exert over the total research effort because of their role in gaining recognition for a particular kind of policy research and researcher, and thus displacing others. The impact on the independent researcher of pressure to work within these relationships should not be discounted.

In the English context there are some illuminating examples of the kind of research that has been sponsored by policy makers, and the uses to which it has been put. A key area here is school effectiveness research, described by Brown et al. (1995) as 'the policy-maker's tool for school improvement'. They explain the attractiveness of school effectiveness to policy makers as resulting from the prospect it offers of identifying the characteristics of effective schools and then using them to improve less effective schools. They argue that there is a particular, well established view of the factors contributing to effectiveness that appeals to policy makers because it reflects their own view of how things should happen, i.e. from the top down. This is the five-factor model (strong educational leadership, emphasis on basic skills, an orderly and secure environment, high expectations of pupil attainment and frequent assessment of pupil progress). This is a top-down model that assumes that if the formal organization is appropriate, then teaching, learning and everything else will follow.

Alternative ways of thinking about school improvement, and, indeed, different research findings that emphasize classroom practices and differences between departments, have had little impact on top-down thinking. For Brown et al., the key issue is that the teachers are left out of the research design, which reflects the priorities and assumptions of policy makers and researchers. They argue that this absence seriously limits the potential of the research model, and, importantly, prevents the future translation of effectiveness from one school to another: 'the involvement and commitment of teachers, with a sense of ownership and responsibility for decision-making, is an essential element for innovation' (Brown et al. 1995: 10).

The authors identify a number of major issues of difference between school effectiveness and school improvement, which make policy makers' assumptions that one can be translated into the other seem misguided. School effectiveness studies focus on readily measurable outcomes (especially examination scores) and on generalizable findings. School improvement studies look at individual institutions in order to develop an understanding of the processes of change that have led to improvement in that school. School effectiveness measures improvement through competition with other schools; school improvement is interested in the school's performance in all kinds of goals. Brown et al. express frustration in attempting to convey these concerns:

> Policy-makers may, of course, regard all this as simply a pedantic diversion on the part of researchers, and no good reason to abandon notions

of making use of clear-cut effectiveness findings for improvement purposes. The trouble is that the findings are not clear cut; they display the complexities and uncertainties that are a characteristic of real schools. A school's overall performance can change significantly over two or three years, its effects can be different for children of different ethnic or social backgrounds, gender or abilities; academic effectiveness may not be associated with social effectiveness; and, as we have already mentioned, much (if not most) of the variation in performance results from effects at classroom rather than school level. Add to these the fact that education seems to account for, at best, 10 to 15% of the variance in pupil performance (substantially less than family and community background variables) and one gets a sense of what 'not clear-cut' means.

(Brown *et al.* 1995: 10)

There are many more examples of the ways in which research for policy seeks simple statements about complex issues. As we have already seen, policy makers seek solutions to problems, and they are inevitably attracted by research that appears generalizable – so that they can implement a 'solution' across the country. They are also often driven towards research that looks 'scientific', particularly if it has generated large amounts of data. The differences between the school effectiveness research and school improvement research, and policy makers' apparent inability to engage with these differences, follow from the large-scale and highly specific nature of effectiveness studies, contrasted with the individual cases that characterize much school improvement research. Further, as Goldstein (1998) has argued, policy makers are attracted to simple, quantitative models of research design that appear scientific but are, in fact, often misleading and unreliable. What is more, they tend to opt for these models even when complex realities can be modelled and applied in ways that may be widely understood. That brings us to the issue of methodologies in education policy research.

Some methodological resources

What follows is not a guide to social research – that would take another book. Instead I set out some of the ways in which methodological choices may be made by someone with an interest in pursuing policy research, broadly defined. The methodological resources that I explore here are generally in keeping with the overall arguments in the book, which have to do with following a *project* in doing research, and with striving for explicitness about the choices that have to be made in doing research on policy.

I cannot set out a range of methodological approaches and methods in the classic manner of a research handbook, and offer them to you as undifferentiated resources, or toolkits for particular tasks. That is because the important choices seem to me to be about purpose and orientation in research, and these tend to construct – or at least indicate – the methodological repertoire. So the important methodological issues for me are to do with connecting the research orientation to data collection and analysis in a coherent and consistent way, and making those connections explicit. They are also about opening up those processes to scrutiny and debate. It may be that there are aspects of these processes that take a particular shape in the context of education policy research, and I look at some methodological problems that may be raised by the nature of research on policy; for example, because of the sensitivity of an issue, and difficulties about access to insider information.

It will be no surprise to learn that this treatment of methodology follows from, and is connected to, earlier discussions of values, ethics and theories, and of the positioning of the researcher in relation to policy research. Methodology, in my view, cannot be separated from these issues, unless a technicist approach is adopted, in which researchers remain outside the social world and maintain a distance from it as a subject of study, in order to achieve objectivity. This is 'hygienic research', with which I am not engaged in this discussion, as I believe that its central premise is mistaken, and that only through our own self-conscious engagement with the social world do we achieve understanding. As Bourdieu (1993: 11) puts it, 'If the sociologist manages to produce any truth, he does so not *despite* the interest he has in producing that truth but *because* he has an interest in doing so – which is the exact opposite of the usual fatuous discourse about "neutrality".'

Linking theory and methodology

In the process of doing policy research in education, data will be collected in some form (and there are many). There are a number of arguments about why researchers collect data, and about what they think they are doing when they collect them. We may collect data because they might refute or support our theorizing, or, if we adopt a grounded theory approach, because they might suggest our theorizing to us. Grounded theory does not work from abstract or general social theories, but starts from observation and the collection of data, which then generate propositions (Glaser and Strauss 1967). There is, then, a close and important relationship between theory and data, but it is a variable one. May (1997) distinguishes inductive and deductive links between theory and data collection: induction relies on the observation of some aspect of social life and the derivation of theory from resultant data; deduction places the theory first and uses observation to confirm or refute the theory.

My objections to induction are, once again, related to explicitness and choice, as it is difficult to see how grounded theorizing can escape completely from framing by pre-theoretical assumptions held by the researcher; the interests of the researcher will shape the content and direction of the research. Processes of deduction are also open to the criticism that they mistake the social world for a scientific laboratory; that is, they rely on notions of falsification to confirm or deny the truth of a particular theoretical hypothesis. This seems to oversimplify the complexity of the kinds of data we are dealing with, and also places the values and orientations of the researcher outside the framework of enquiry. The existence of some underlying rules or principles of social organization to be discovered 'out there' is also, I feel, implied by inductive theorizing.

As I indicated above, we can return to the theoretical resources discussed in Chapter 3 as a way of coming to terms with the kinds of choices we need to make in the collection and interpretation of evidence. If we remain committed to the idea that knowledge is produced in certain conditions and relationships, then the important issue becomes the ways in which that knowledge production is subjected to democratic scrutiny and participation. Here we link to critical theory, as articulated earlier by Cox, in which we close the gap between facts and values and seek to challenge inequitable social relations by doing research that challenges oppression:

> At the heart of critical social research is the idea that knowledge is structured by existing sets of social relations. The aim of a critical methodology is to provide knowledge which engages the prevailing social structures. These social structures are seen by critical social researchers, in one way or another, as oppressive structures.
>
> (Harvey 1990: 2)

Feminist research on policy

I want to use the example of feminist research to illustrate, very sharply, the ways in which processes of knowledge production (including research) can themselves act as oppressive structures. I am not conflating feminism and critical theory, though there may be alignment, and I am mindful of the existence of feminisms, both in general (Humm 1992) and in education (Weiner 1996). However, the example of feminism and its place in knowledge production is instructive.

The starting point for this discussion is feminist theory, which draws our attention to patriarchy and demands an orientation to research that seeks to challenge patriarchal assumptions and explanations. There are considerable implications for research methodology that follow from a feminist research orientation or perspective. These go beyond the recognition of the absence of women from social theory as knowledge producers, and the further recognition that men in the academy have used power to discourage women from participating on equal terms in knowledge production. As well as noting the injustice of this, there is the consequence for theorizing and research about the social world that defines society and its problems and issues predominantly through masculine perspectives. It is also worth pointing out that those perspectives could include assumptions about the subordination of women that are sustained by this form of enquiry and by the masculine domination of the academy.

Methodologies that seek to challenge all these assumptions have been developed within feminist research, and, although there are differences in emphasis, there is considerable agreement about the need to challenge perspectives on social life that encapsulate assumptions about normal or natural subordination of women. Because 'normal' enquiry has been so exclusively masculine in its assumptions, it follows that women are largely absent or spoken for in gender-blind theory and literature. In methodological terms, then, one of the key aims of feminist research was/is to collect and disseminate women's voices and thus to challenge their exclusion. Going further, feminist theorists and researchers argued that 'adding on' women to existing bodies of knowledge was not sufficient: that what were needed were feminist epistemologies and ontologies; in other words, ways in which we perceive the world and know the world that were distinctively feminist.

Methodologically this produced very interesting developments, particularly in feminist standpoint theory. This takes the position that women's exclusion from power and from the public realm is a research advantage, because women are consequently able to operate simultaneously from the informed (and privileged) position of scholarship and from the oppressed standpoint of women. Experience is thus recognized by the feminist standpoint researcher as reflecting dominant social relationships; experience is the critical area of enquiry for research; and the fractured and fragmented experiences of women provide an appropriate way of understanding social reality. Appropriate attention to experience leads to research methods that enable experience to be shared, reflected upon and absorbed. Respect for experience and the shared experience of oppression demand equality of status between the researcher and those with whom she is conducting the enquiry.

Feminist standpoint methodology is likely to involve interviewing, as opposed to the technicist and distant processes implied in 'administering' a questionnaire, which places control of the enquiry in the hands of the researcher. Methods are likely to involve personal interaction and negotiation of agreement about meaning. Disengagement is not appropriate, and research methods that structure and shape or distort interaction between the people engaged in the research process are unlikely to be adopted. To a degree this method reflects the ways in which many women interact, as Finch (1984) points out. Women are more used than men to questions about their lives, from official persons (doctors, health workers), but also from friends, while their experience in the 'privatised, domestic sphere . . . makes it particularly likely that they will welcome the opportunity to talk to a sympathetic listener' (Finch 1984: 74).

This has certainly been my own experience in pursuing research with women, even outside the privatized, domestic sphere. I briefly discuss that work, with the main aim of illustrating one way of trying to put these feminist research principles into practice, but I hope that the discussion also illustrates ways of relating theory to data, and offers some further ideas about what constitutes research in education policy.

Using women to manage the unmanageable: is this policy?

This research was carried out by myself and Rosemary Deem with the assistance of Jocey Quinn, during 1995–6, and is reported in a number of publications (Ozga and Deem 1996; Deem and Ozga 1997). The research process involved telephone interviews with women senior managers in further and higher education. They were identified through personal contacts that we already had, who then put us in touch with more potential interviewees; this is sometimes called the 'snowball' method of building up appropriate contacts. This was not a random exercise that involved sampling across the population of female managers; we did not do that because we wanted to talk to women managers who would describe themselves as feminists. This was because the subject of our enquiry was the presumed tension between the pressures of managerialism and the agenda for greater equality and for the challenge to patriarchy that these women had identified with.

Going further, we were interested in exploring the idea that women's people management skills were being recognized and rewarded because they were very useful in ensuring the acquiescence of those for whom they were responsible in situations that contained much potential for conflict; for example, where student numbers were increasing and resources diminishing.

The research topic is a policy issue, in the terms in which we have understood policy in this book. In particular, it provides a focus on managerialism in further and higher education, and raises questions about institutional responses to policy imperatives of efficiency and expansion. The focus on gender provides a corrective to the gender-blindness of much policy research, and raises new issues. These include the nature of the relationship between an increased female presence in positions of power in further and higher education (FHE) and the general orientation of policy in these sectors. Is the relationship coincidental, reflecting women's greater representation in senior levels produced by changes in attitude? Or is there a happy or 'designed' coincidence that works for policy makers?

These are policy issues, and they relate to broader changes in women's employment in the public sector, and the apparent increase in opportunities for promotion for women there, not just in the UK, but elsewhere. I would ask if it is possible to interpret this as a consequence of greater equality in the workplace, and I would be cautious about that because of the timing of these promotions (they become available to women just as the jobs themselves become extremely problematic). I am also interested in the fact that so many women are moving into middle management posts in the FHE sector, while the very senior management positions remain almost exclusively occupied by men. Since I understand managerialism as a very important element in the redesign of educational institutions, so that they are more effective carriers and transmitters of economized education, I am led to thinking about why these promotions should be happening now, and what kinds of effects they are having on the people gaining them. Such questioning relates to policy dimensions at the level of the institution and at the more abstract level of changes in work more generally, which help the new project of institutional redesign for managerial imperatives.

Interviewing feminist managers allows for some quite explicit engagement with these concerns, through exploring what they thought they were doing when they became managers, what their purposes were, whether they have adhered to them, what problems they have encountered and so on. The methodology involved the drawing up of a schedule of areas of enquiry that we wanted to discuss with the women managers. These were very much aimed at eliciting discussion of experience. Starting from background, we moved into (self) description, including aspects of their feminism, policy areas such as increasing access and representativeness in the student population, experiences of management and its changes, experience of men and women managers, the social relations of work and the impact of the work on their identities. In pursuit of these questions we offered opportunity for dialogue; as we (the researchers) had experiences as managers and as feminists that could be offered in exchanges about these topics, so the process of obtaining and analysing data was very much a process of discussion and (mutual) recognition of experience. We believe that this allowed us to gather material in this area that was very frank and honest about the experience of senior management in education in the current context, and that was not over-preoccupied with ensuring a highly efficient and 'managed' self-presentation.

Almost all the women we interviewed were aware of their role as cultural change agents, and many thought that it was better to take the opportunities this presented than to leave it to men. Feminist women's ideas about the most appropriate forms of change, and their emphasis on equity, trust, negotiation and collaboration, all of which were strongly evidenced in the interviews, were not necessarily shared by their male colleagues or part of a managerialist discourse, though it may invoke them as rhetoric. Our interviewees tended to think that women managed differently from men. These are examples of statements that illustrate that view:

Women generally work more collaboratively and independently and have a more caring approach. It's a less paranoid style of management, you don't have to be seen to be upfront all the time, but you get on with things.

(Programme director, FE)

I do think women manage differently from men . . . we tend to negotiations and diplomacy. I worry more about stress levels. I get on very well with my male colleagues though. I'm much less prestige conscious and much more optimistic. I think ultimately you can find ways of doing things. You can usually implement and exploit them to do the minimal damage and take people with you.

(Centre director, FE)

In relation to the central research question of the ways in which women managers implemented and interpreted managerialism, the research produced mixed evidence. On the one hand, the feminist women managers we spoke to all retained a strong commitment to equal opportunities policies that they illustrated with reference to their actions in a number of areas; for example, in promotions, appointments and student recruitment. However, they also provided evidence of tension between the new policy imperatives and these commitments, as well as tension between these imperatives and their preferred management style. This was more marked in FE than in HE. FE has become more business-like in recent years: old departmental cultures have been replaced by flexible managers who are designated team leaders, project heads and coordinators. The funding mechanism for FE has been designed to increase input, output and throughput, and seeks standardization and reduction of costs. Colleges are funded to help young people to improve their skills and career prospects; much of the activity that concerned recreational education, or leisure or citizenship education, is no longer offered in the sector as it no longer qualifies for funding. It is against that context, and the emergence of sharp distinctions between the flexible workforce of part-time teachers and the permanent staff of managers, that we can see the likelihood of tension in the accounts of the women managers. Here is one very sharp example:

It's not exactly my favourite job for life. Were I not fifty I would change career. Women are being used in this climate as managers in FE, that is something I would like to say. Quite a few women senior managers are being used to bulldoze the terrible changes because they're desperate to get on and they've never been offered promotion before, and because you don't recognise a poisoned chalice when it's offered to you.

(Programme manager, FE)

Against this type of comment, we need to remember those who stress the new opportunities:

I think it's a very recent change. I can remember when I was at college I don' t think there were any women managers. It's a good thing women can see their way upwards rather than sideways, it's not impossible for you to be a principal. It's been a change for the better.

(Programme manager, FE)

The shared experience of interviewers and interviewees allowed our respondents to talk to us freely about some of the problems they encountered in their work, and what the experience of work felt like for them. Many of the women wanted to stress their enjoyment of the challenges and potential of the job, but also gave us insights into the costs of this kind of work, particularly where they felt isolated in masculine cultures:

In an organisation like this you wouldn't bare your soul to your colleagues . . . there's a considerable amount of rivalry between directors, we have to watch our reputations.

(Section director, FE)

I sometimes think it would be nice to have a wife to go home to.

(Section director, FE)

male management is very unhappy with criticism or critique, and it gets very defensive and sneery . . . I wish there were more of us . . . The baggage you carry around, it doesn't get any easier . . . you feel you fight the same battles on a regular basis.

(Associate dean, former polytechnic)

I find it a very lonely job in some ways, positioned between the Dean and heads of departments . . . I feel I can't let myself get too close . . . Exclusionary tactics are used against women, not conscious, but they operate.

(Assistant dean, former polytechnic)

The conversations with feminist women managers provide information that is rich, detailed and complex. As you will have already recognized, this material is quite hard to analyse in relation to the research issues that prompted the research. Of course, we could have done a survey that would have forced the respondents to choose a position, or we could have used some measurement of attitude, and thus simplified the task of analysis. However, we believed that we would have lost the complexity of our material, which is, we think, an accurate representation of reality.

So how does one reach a conclusion about the research question in the face of this varied evidence? My own inclination was to read these texts as evidence of co-option into economically driven agendas of the kind that Yeatman (1990: 341) describes: 'Equal opportunity in this context comes to be reframed in terms of what it can do for management improvement, not in terms of what it can do to develop the conditions of social justice and democratic citizenship.' Jill Blackmore also stresses the opportunities for managerialism presented by the growth of numbers of women in management:

> Women's 'propensity' for more democratic modes of decision making, their emotional management skills derived out of their familial and pedagogic experiences, and their emphasis on curriculum and student welfare is [*sic*] an exploitable resource for new styles of management.
>
> (Blackmore 1995: 49)

In this reading of the evidence, the conclusion offered is as follows:

> We conclude that any coincidence of women's preferred styles as managers, the predominant organisational cultures in tertiary education and the processes sustained by the new managerial discourses must be viewed critically, as the apparent connections may become ties that bind women to their institutions, thereby contributing to surface amelioration of the unacceptable. But awareness of this danger, and of the complexity facing feminist women managers in these difficult times assists in the process of negotiating 'positionality', and of acceptance that 'one's subjectivity is . . . necessarily contradictory' (Davies 1992: 3). Working through the contradictions this presents, in a principled, yet pragmatic fashion, becomes a central task for the feminist manager. Their presence in these organisations at least indicates the possibility that such activity may happen.
>
> (Ozga and Deem 1996: 12)

Deem and Ozga (1997) put the emphasis more heavily on the capacity of feminists to pursue their agendas in a complex and contradictory period of change.

What does this convey about research methodology? I would argue, first, that the exemplification of feminist research shows the advantages to be gained from pursuing its precepts in the data gathering and interpretive stages of research (and it should be noted that these are not, in practice, watertight compartments in this kind of research). Shared experience provided a necessary basis for the development of exchanges in which ambivalence and difficulty were recorded. More generally, the example illustrates the gains made by gathering rich biographical, subjective and reflective data. It also illustrates the problems that arise in interpreting or analysing such data, as they do not fall neatly into categories, nor can they be reduced to numerical equivalents and subjected to mathematically based analytic techniques. We were careful, in our analysis of data, to agree categories into which we thought they fell, and to discuss their interpretation, particularly by referring to the complete 'story' told to us by each interviewee, and its contextualization in the institutional culture. The very slight differences in interpretation that I think come through in a reading of the associated publications probably have more to do with the 'lacework of meaning' of each researcher, discussed above. Perhaps we should each have offered our own accounts of our experience of management and the impact it had made on our reading of possibilities and constraints.

The analysis of qualitative data (that is, data gathered from interviews, observations and so on, rather than quantifiable indicators) is one of the most difficult areas of methodology. There is plenty of good advice about how to do qualitative research, but gathering data seems to be covered in rather more detail than data analysis. Details of data analysis are quite sparse in research reporting. This can lead to difficulties where other researchers are seeking to pursue arguments raised by research findings, and cannot see clearly how the process of analysis was carried out. Methodological controversies here may, of course, be fronts for fundamental disagreements about how research should be done. We have already seen how the issue of school choice became a focus for controversy about how researcher orientation to a policy issue impacted on research choices. Here I want to look at the same protagonists and their disputes over methodology.

Methodological controversies

The discussion of feminist research was intended to highlight the extent to which a particular orientation to research can shape the research design, from the choice of topic through the process of data gathering and into the process of analysis and dissemination of findings. Of course, these are chains of consequences that apply not only to feminist research; but perhaps feminist research is most explicit in its engagement with them. Critical theorists (who may be feminists) challenge the separation of facts from experiences and attempt to contribute, through research, to a project in which the relations of domination are exposed, in order that they may be challenged, and no longer buttressed by common-sense assumptions that are themselves the product of the operation of political and economic power (Gramsci 1971).

In this section I return to a controversy that I discussed earlier in the book, namely the dispute between Tooley (1997) and Gewirtz *et al.* (1995) about research on markets in education. In the earlier discussion I was concerned to explore the ways in which the orientations of the researchers led them into irreconcilable differences, in which methodological issues stood proxy for ideological ones. I now want to look at the methodological points raised by Tooley in more detail, because they are of interest in relation to the debate on research for policy that he has contributed to through ERAC, and because they illustrate key issues in methodological debates.

Tooley takes issue with the research published in *Markets, Choice and Equity* on the grounds that the qualitative method cannot support the generalization about class and choice which is made (i.e. that there is a relationship between social class and school choice). He also mounts a critique of the operationalization of the research concepts used, in particular the analytical process through which the data are understood and conceptualized. I am discussing this case in detail because it illustrates clearly the different assumptions that underlie different research traditions. Just as Tooley is at odds with Gewirtz *et al.* about the meaning of the market in education, as we saw, so too the differences about methodology are not really about technical questions but about assumptions about what research is for and how it may be done. As Ball and Gewirtz put it, in their response to Tooley's critique, 'his ideological and social theoretical perspectives lead him to see the social world in a rather different way' (Ball and Gewirtz 1997: 584).

Tooley makes two main points in his critique, and these are that generalizations should not be drawn from qualitative research, and that the categorizations of families on which their data analysis is based are not replicable because they are unclear and inconsistently applied. Throughout the discussion, Tooley uses the language of positivistic research as a basis for finding fault with work that it quite explicitly not in that tradition. For example, he talks about 'sample size', 'statistical machinery' and generalization. He also provides an interesting comment on what he understands as the appropriate role of qualitative research: 'a perfectly legitimate function of qualitative work . . . is to fill in the human detail behind previous quantitative work, or even behind hypotheses not yet empirically tested' (Tooley 1997: 229). This illustrates nicely the very traditional view of qualitative and quantitative research apparently held by Tooley, in which there is a necessary separation of function between the two that depends on the measurement of trends in the objective external world (by quantitative research) and the addition of human colour through qualitative research. This dichotomizing of qualitative and quantitative methods depends on adherence to the view that the social world is transparently 'real', and offers only a secondary role to people's perceptions and experiences. As Ball and Gewirtz (1997) point out, Tooley has chosen to misunderstand the focus of their research; they were concerned to explore processes (i.e. how was it that families with shared concerns for the welfare of their children ended up making different kinds of choices?).

The other argument raised by Tooley concerns the issue of generalization, and here he seems to be making the argument that generalizations should not be made from qualitative data. These arguments are also made by Tooley in his influential report on research (ERAC) discussed above. They are important because they are influencing the discussion of educational research and its relationship to policy.

Once again, I would suggest that the arguments being advanced here are more to do with two views of the world, and of how we best understand it, than with any inherent difference between qualitative and quantitative research. As I have already stated, the choice between such methods depends, for me, on the kind of data that are sought, and there is often potential in research design for a mix of the two. However, what is in contention here is a view of educational enquiry that understands 'objective' data as real, and subjective data as illustrative. Only hard, concrete, real data have status in this view, and they may be subjected to analysis by 'statistical machinery'. Large sample size and statistical technique, in this view, enable results to be reliable and valid, and so justify their use in informing policy, because they describe what is really happening. If we return to the research issue in question, processes of school choice, and think about the application of a 'scientific' design to this research problem, we can begin to see where differences and difficulties arise.

In the first place, the processes of choice in all their ambivalence and messiness, as recorded by Gewirtz *et al.*, would be largely invisible to forms of enquiry that demand unambiguous responses in order to allow them to be analysed using statistical techniques. Almost all such models produce conceptual simplicity in categorization, even where there is considerable technical complexity in analysis. This does not have to be the case, but, as Goldstein (1998: 7) comments, it very often is:

> it is really quite difficult to provide mathematical or statistical models which do begin to approach the complexity of the real world, and even when this can be done, the costs of obtaining adequate data to test out these models is very high. This is, however, no excuse for perpetrating inadequate models as if they were realistic descriptions. My own view is that such promotion has been an important cause of the polarization within education, and the social sciences more generally, between the quantitative and qualitative schools of research. Yet, to argue against the over-selling of certain simplistic views of the world, is not to argue against the use of quantitative methods. On the contrary, the use of quantitative methodologies which are rich enough to match the real complexities of the social world may eventually allow us to bridge the gap between qualitative understandings which emphasize these complexities, and quantitative tools and understandings which provide formal descriptions of them which can be operated upon to obtain testable propositions, further refinements and useful generalisations.

If we consider our earlier discussion, it may be that this dispute over methodology reveals a number of layers of irreconcilable difference about the orientation of the protagonists to educational research. These differences are played out in the repertoire of choices that they make in doing the research and in interpreting it. And behind these differences of orientation lie very fundamental differences about how choice is related to opportunity in society. For Tooley, engagement with the market offers enhancement of potential, as the conclusion to his *Education without the State* makes clear:

> With a lowered school-leaving age and funds in a LIFE account, young people could at last begin to express their genuine educational needs and requirements; with private funds invested, enterprise and initiative creatively harnessed, a diversity of schools and other educational opportunities could emerge to serve this demand. But the proposals do not force change if change is not desired. They are not imposing 'the dogma of the market' on anyone, only allowing the market to cultivate an environment in which educational needs can be discovered and development nurtured. Most importantly, the proposals do not take us towards something to be feared. Markets in education are justified in terms of equity and democracy. For too long government intervention has deadened and subdued the enterprise of education. Moving towards markets will enliven and liberate the educational endeavour.
>
> (Tooley 1996: 110–11)

For Tooley, then, the research data produced by Gewirtz *et al.* may be reinterpreted to produce results favourable to his position on markets. Implicit in his critique is the argument that the researchers' ideological convictions have skewed their analysis of their data. My argument here is that he is himself caught by this critique, in his own reading of their data.

Tooley argues that the solution to such research problems lies in avoiding generalization based on specific, illuminative research and in making the process of analysis transparent. I would suggest that the arguments about exposing the principles of choice in research design are a preferable alternative. The argument about avoiding generalization is, as we have seen, based on a misconception that there is a fundamental difference in the nature of the truth claims that can be made for different kinds of research. However, clarification of all the processes that contribute to choice in the research allows for the research to be 'read' clearly and transparently. Ball and Gewirtz (1997) make the point in their rejoinder to Tooley that they are basing their investigation of processes on a large literature that connects social class and school choice. What they are perhaps insufficiently explicit about is the way in which their project is shaped by theoretical resources that attempt to set out how class is enacted in consumption more generally, and that deal with the capacity to discriminate as the acquisition of socially differentiated dispositions that are class related. They do refer to Bourdieu in building their arguments that the typology of choosers they develop is class related. They write: 'In Bourdieu's terms, the market constitutes a particular cultural arbitrary which presupposes "possession of the cultural code required for the decoding of the objects displayed"' (Gewirtz *et al.* 1995).

This and other references to Bourdieu do not really convey adequately the extent of the resource offered to the researchers in terms of thinking about how social and cultural capital and its possession or lack may work with the processes of choice to reinforce existing class advantage/disadvantage. There is, as I have noted elsewhere, with colleagues (Menter *et al.* 1997), a reluctance in research in education in England to declare its theory-led choices, and a commitment to letting the data generate the theory. As I stated above, I think that there are problems with this approach, because it tends to echo the notion that the researcher is 'out' of the frame, operating hygienically, and that data are likely to generate meanings, which seems to me to come close to positivistic assumptions about underlying rules of social organization, waiting to be uncovered. Once again, I would prefer the enunciation of the principle of choice as a means of ensuring the correct understanding of the claims being made for research.

Another example of theory-led research: textual analysis

I have noted that I cannot provide a comprehensive review of methods of data collection and analysis; instead, I am reviewing and discussing some methods that are familiar to me (mainly because I have used them) and/or seem likely to be productive in a framework that seeks to build explicitness about research choices. Here I want to discuss the analysis of policy 'texts'. Discussion and analysis of text is a useful method in policy research; much policy text is publicly available and readily accessible, and policy texts make it possible to examine policy over time.

I should perhaps make it clear that I am not here writing about 'policy as text' in the sense used by Stephen Ball (1993). In that discussion, Ball suggests that policy may be conceptualized as 'text' and as 'discourse'. He further maintains that these are distinct categories: 'two very different conceptualisations of policy' (Ball 1993: 10). Policy as text is the element of policy that can be worked on, interpreted and contextualized, and stands in contradiction to assumptions that policy works in a straight line from formulation to implementation. Policy as discourse understands policy as part of the dominant system of social relations; policy as discourse frames what can be said or thought. Policy as text addresses agency, policy as discourse addresses structure. In passing, I agree with Henry's (1993) comment that it is hard to see why these categories should be dichotomous rather than relational: text and discourse surely operate in relation to one another. If they are relational, then it is hard to see why they should be conceptualized differently. Whatever the rights or wrongs of that debate, it is not the subject here. In this discussion of policy texts, they are seen as a resource for analysis in terms of the messages they convey – or seek to convey – about the following issues.

- *The source of the policy*: whose interests it serves; its relationship to global, national and local imperatives.
- *The scope of the policy*: what it is assumed it is able to do; how it frames the issues; the policy relationships embedded in it.
- *The pattern of the policy*: what it builds on or alters in terms of relationships, what organizational and institutional changes or developments it requires.

I think it is also useful to think about policy texts as carrying particular narratives; that is, they tell a story about what is possible or desirable to achieve through education policy. They are thus able to be read as any narrative is read: they may be scrutinized for their portrayal of character and plot, for their use of particular forms of language in order to produce impressions or responses; they may have an authorial 'voice' or seek to convey the impression of multiple viewpoints.

There is a distinction to be made between formal policy texts and texts that we, as researchers, choose to interpret as policy texts. What I am trying to say is that we should not restrict our understanding of texts to those that come with 'policy text' stamped all over them; for example, White and Green Papers, Bills and Acts of Parliament, regulations governing decision-making at all levels of provision, policy documents in institutions setting out guidelines for practice in relation to disability or admissions or promotion or whatever. Nor should we restrict ourselves to other forms of 'formal' data, such as descriptions of significant facts; for example, budget statements or statements of desirable outcomes (policy for something). I would like to extend the category of policy text to include documentary or other materials that can be read as significant within the discursive parameters of an investigation, provided that detailed justification is given for their inclusion. Such thinking greatly extends the category of policy text. The disadvantage for my present purposes is that I cannot provide a clear basis for the selection of texts, but I hope that the flexibility of the category allows for imaginative interpretation that goes beyond the formal categories used by policy analysts and towards the kinds of illuminative work done by historians and cultural analysts.

An example may be useful here, and I draw again from my experience.

Policy texts and social exclusion/inclusion

After the New Labour election victory in May 1997, some attention was given by policy makers to the issue of increased inequality following from the introduction of markets into public sector services like health and education. Although markets were accepted, there was a search for new ways of ensuring that the most disadvantaged were not 'excluded' from basic entitlements by the operation of market mechanisms, and at the same time (though less obviously) there was a concern to prevent the 'exit' from public service provision of elites who could purchase further advantage.

These policy concerns prompted interest from education policy researchers, and suggested a number of areas of research. It is possible to argue, from a critical social science perspective, that the issue of equality and its enhancement or reduction through education remains the key topic for research. The introduction of markets, and the associated significant changes in the steering mechanisms of the state, provided significant opportunities in theory to explore the relationship between different forms of governance and different incidences of inequality. In the same way, the apparent 'globalization' of policy raised questions about the capacity of nation states to develop 'local' solutions to growing problems of inequality, and offered opportunities for comparison of the impact of global agendas and changes in forms of governance on local cultures of provision.

There are, obviously, many ways in which such topics could be explored. A social science project might see research as necessary in areas such as:

- assessing changes in the overall rate of inequality in education provision (these would include inequalities of opportunity conceptualized as access, inequalities of outcome and inequalities of experience);
- investigating, through the development of theory and enquiry, the possible relationships between changes in governance and changed rates of inclusion/exclusion in education;
- attempting accurate analyses of new forms of educational governance;
- obtaining detailed descriptions of the experiences of exclusion and inclusion in education;
- developing ways of theorizing about inclusion and exclusion;
- finding ways of challenging increases in exclusion (if they are shown to exist) through documentation of the processes and advocacy of changes in policy.

A policy analysis project on a similar theme might take a rather different form. In particular, the focus would be on combating exclusion, and research would probably begin at that end of the spectrum of possibilities. We can see this approach in the establishment of the Social Exclusion Unit within the Cabinet Office in the UK, and in developments aimed at 'joined up' or third way policy making, where different services and sectors are brought together to combat exclusionary pressures not just in education, but in health, employment and community development; for example, in the Education Action Zones (EAZs). I am not suggesting that these projects are of no value or use to people who need help, but I am arguing that the analyses they develop may be limited and so the solutions they propose may be ameliorative rather than fundamental. Research *for* policy relating to social exclusion takes certain aspects of the policy agenda as immutable;

these include globalization and policy responses to it, elements of public private partnership, rather than planned state intervention, and the economizing agenda as a significant element in the solution to these problems.

Research *on* policy in this area is more able to take a critical view of policy in response to globalization and the economizing of education as potential contributors to exclusion. It is also more likely to have a concern for the future of national state systems and for scrutiny of their contribution to formations of identity and culture. For policy makers, the national interest is limited to gaining competitive advantage in a globalizing economy. Social scientists, preoccupied with the fragmentation of social life and the emergence of new forms of stratification in network cultures (Castells 1997) seek to raise the political and social implications of economic development and to understand them fully. In the case of research on social exclusion and educational governance, there may be areas of overlap between research for and research on policy, depending on the kinds of policy contextual factors in research funding that we discussed above. It is likely, for example, that the DfEE funded programme of evaluation of the EAZs will impose some constraints on researchers, and may well be restricted in terms of selection of researchers deemed appropriate for such work. New rules for contract researchers working for the DfEE stipulate that when they submit detailed drafts of reports before publication they *must* accept amendments to them.

My involvement in research on social exclusion and inclusion came through participation in a European Union funded project on the impact of new forms of educational governance on social exclusion and inclusion in nine nation states. The research project is both social science research and policy analysis, as the funding body undoubtedly seeks advice on policy that can be translated into action to assist in combating exclusion. The project members were all social scientists with a greater or lesser proximity to policy, depending on their national contexts. The interest of the researchers bridged the social science–policy gap, but this was possible because there were few pressures on the project team to work in particular ways. There were constraints of time and money, and the reporting procedures required by Brussels to a degree shaped the pattern of the research. However, the intellectual resources brought to bear by the group, and its preoccupation with finding good theoretical tools for examining governance and exclusion, ensured that its research activities were not limited to research for policy.

The project team used a number of forms of enquiry, including interviews with policy makers at all levels of the system ('system actors'), interviews with excluded young people, investigation of official data that measured exclusion/inclusion (for example, educational data such as staying on rates at different critical points of transition in provision, examination passes and more general social data on health, welfare and employment), the reanalysis of data sets on young people and crime, unemployment, low achievement and so on. In addition, we tried to find ways of studying the story about inclusion/exclusion that different societies told about their education systems: the sagas or myths about education that shaped assumptions about the scope of education. These seemed to us to be significant in testing the reality of 'globalization', and to connect to ideas about the pattern of education having a continuing effect on new policy developments, however far-reaching and irresistible they might seem.

As part of that investigation, each participating country's research team produced an account of its system and the ways in which the story told related to exclusion and inclusion. Different stories emerged, some of rational progress, others of disputes between groups on the basis of religious, ethnic or national/regional difference. In order to pursue these ideas further, we also undertook an investigation of key policy texts that would contribute something to understanding of governance and exclusion/inclusion. Once again, we are brought back to the issue of choice, as it will be readily apparent that systems produce many more policy texts than could possibly be analysed. Choices of text had to be justified.

The project team also identified analytical parameters to guide work on the textual analysis. Because we were attempting to do comparative work, a framework of this kind was necessary, or we would not have been able to read the texts across the different national cases. We chose to work with 'common-sense' categories of policy text, but also deliberately to seek something more unconventional, with the intention of assisting us in devising new forms of understanding of exclusion/inclusion. After all, we were doing the project at this time to investigate what was claimed to be a new situation. Texts were therefore selected that dealt directly with both governance and exclusion/inclusion. These texts also needed to be concerned with educational reform and restructuring processes that were already 'out there' in the policy literature and in policy itself. Three areas were therefore adopted:

- *Clients*: subjects or groups that are deemed by policy makers in official documents as in need of attention.
- *Organization*: to include budget, personnel and management issues.
- *Curriculum*: not just in its narrow sense of subjects prescribed, but also assumptions about purpose and outcome of study, ethos, pedagogy, etc.

These texts had to be in some sense 'representative' of their systems. For England there were many useful possibilities: the government's documentation for the EAZ initiative, for example, or the White Paper *Excellence in Schools*. Texts for Scotland (which was the subject of a separate case study, as it has a distinctive education system and a separate government department for the administration of education – the Scottish Office Education and Industry Department – and now has a separate Parliament with jurisdiction over Scottish affairs, including education policy) included the SOEID website. This 'text', though 'conventional' in the project's terms, raises interesting questions in itself about the nature of governance and exclusion/exclusion (Who has access? What messages are transmitted through this medium, and to whom?).

The selection of 'unconventional' texts was challenging. We were looking for a text that could be analysed in detail, that was not self-evidently 'about' the research topic, but nevertheless highly instructive for understanding significant shifts in what was understood as 'normal'. An example that might convey the intention was to investigate the visitors to the DfEE in a given period, to explore who they were, where they came from and why. The point of exploring this 'text' (in effect, the DfEE visitors' book) is that it might help to substantiate the impression that the rules of governance were changing; that the field of 'expertise' was being redrawn, that ideas from outside England were being explored, that business and industry were significant actors in these policy shifts, that the policy community was being reconfigured. Other possibilities as 'unconventional' texts would be proposals for teacher education, for example, which is conventionally seen as detached from governance or exclusion/inclusion, but which may well repay study in relation to them.

Texts, once selected, were then analysed following a common framework of questions, once again with the intention of ensuring a common direction of enquiry across the different nation states without assuming that terms like 'governance' had a shared, taken-for-granted meaning across the systems. So, in scrutinizing our chosen texts, we all asked the following questions, which are a selection from the text analysis protocol.

Governance–social exclusion and inclusion
- What ideas and categories are presented in the texts regarding governance? Are these new? In what ways? What is absent, excluded, silent in the account?
- What ideas and categories are presented in the text regarding social exclusion/inclusion? Are these new? In what ways? What is absent, excluded, silent?
- Construction of narrative. What story is being presented here? What kind of story is it, and what images are present in it? Are these new?
- What is the logic/discursive construction of the argument in the text? Is this new?

Citizen–state–world relations
- How does the text construct its subjects? How are teachers and learners constructed, individually and relationally? Are these new?
- Who is excluded by these constructions?
- What do these texts imply about the relationship between their subjects (including the state and civil society here) and the world society/globalization? Is this new?

I turn now to the policy document *Excellence in Schools*, and indicate briefly some of the results of applying that framework to this document. I cannot here produce a complete analysis, but an illustration may help to convince you of the potential of this kind of approach (and it also illustrates some of the issues about interpretation that we have been concerned with up to this point in the discussion).

This document was the first White Paper of the new Labour administration. It represented a new approach to policy making in its form, in that it offers a number of policy principles and policy targets against which the government may be judged, and it is presented as (conventional) text but is also illustrated and supported by a video. I concentrate here on the first section of the White Paper ('A new approach'), which sets out the broad objectives of education policy, the reasons behind them and the ways in which they will be achieved.

Text analysis: governance; what ideas and categories; are these new; how; what silences?

The issue of governance is strongly represented in the introduction to the White Paper. Governance is present in the presentation of government as active, passionate and full of urgency about education, which is 'the Government's top priority' (p. 9). The place of government in the task of producing excellence in schools is a central one; although there are references to 'partnership . . . with all those who share our passion' (p. 9), there is a strong impression that policy is to be government-led. There is an emphasis on legislation, stressing how much has already been introduced in pursuit of the government's aims, and on the increased size and status of the DfEE, and a pledge to increase spending. Outcomes and policies that are central to the achievement of excellence are directly connected to government action. For example, in relation to teachers the following claim is made: 'under this government there will be the right balance of pressure and support which will enable us, together, to rise to the challenges of the new millennium' (p. 11). A further example of government's central role is: 'the government will reduce the extent of early failure in the system by encouraging best practice and effective monitoring with speedy intervention where necessary' (p. 11).

The major actor in policy making is the government. If we look at the more general issue of what meanings of *governance* may be read into this document, then we need to follow through the logic of a strong, central lead by government. Thus, although there are references to partnership, the operation of governance sets government in surveillance and control mode in relation to the various partners, in particular the LEAs and the teachers. I infer this from the ways in which the 'problems we face' are outlined. They depend heavily on acceptance of failure as located within the school system, so that success is seen as attainable within that system, if it is better managed. From this there follows a repertoire of mechanisms that together will ensure better performance; these combine to reflect governance understood as the alteration of people's behaviour through a combination of advocacy and surveillance. This is the meaning of the paragraphs that assert that 'standards matter more than structures', 'intervention will be in inverse proportion to success' and 'there will be zero tolerance of underperformance'. Material in the text that connects to my interpretation of what it says about governance includes the following:

> Effective change in a field as dependent on human interaction as education requires millions of people to change their behaviour. This will require consistent advocacy and persuasion to create a climate in which schools are constantly challenged . . .
>
> Ideally intervention should be preventive and early, so that severe failure is avoided. The Government intends to put in place arrangements for targeted interventions by LEAs or the DfEE, informed by Ofsted, that are appropriate to the scale of the problem.
>
> . . . we shall put in place policies which seek to avoid failure. But where failure occurs, we shall tackle it head on. Schools which have been found to be failing will have to improve, make a fresh start, or close. The principle of zero tolerance will also apply to local education authorities . . . we intend to create an education service in which every school is either excellent, or improving, or both.
>
> Government will lead the drive to raise standards and create the right framework, but it cannot succeed alone. It must work in partnership with all those who have a part to play in improving the quality of education: parents, teachers and governors, local authorities, teachers and business. Parents are a child's primary educator and our partnership approach will involve them fully. We want to put the years of division, conflict and short-term thinking behind us . . .
>
> We will be alert to new ways of working with others to raise standards: new forms of Public/Private Partnership; new forms of collaboration between local and central government; new ways of involving parents in education; new relationships between private and state schools and new ways of involving volunteers and working with voluntary organisations. Our literacy and numeracy targets for 11-year-olds (see chapter 2) for example, are not just targets set by the Government to hold the education service to account; but targets set by the Government and the education service together, for which both are jointly accountable.
>
> (DfEE 1997a: 12)

Although these quotations make reference to partnership, which is not a new idea or category in educational governance, the sense of partnership seems to me to have changed quite markedly from the traditional three-way relationship of department, LEAs and teachers. Partnership is now much more diffuse, embracing the whole community and tying it into the project of improvement. Partnership is also very obviously unequal, as no amount of reference to the shared nature of the project can conceal the very strong tendency to control and direct it from the centre. Responsibility for success (and failure) is diffused throughout the system, but there is, in the tone and tenor of the document, an underlying story of energetic, visionary government with zero tolerance of failure to respond to its vision.

What story is being presented? Is it new? How?

Importantly, the story that supports these versions of governance and government is one of economically driven change. Excellence in education is necessary for economic productivity:

> Education is the key to creating a society which is dynamic and productive, offering opportunity and fairness to all. It is the Government's top priority. We will work in partnership with all those who share our passion and sense of urgency for higher standards.

> Learning can unlock the treasure that lies within us all. In the 21st century, knowledge and skills will be the key to success. Our goal is a society in which everyone is well-educated and able to learn throughout life. Britain's economic prosperity and social cohesion both depend on achieving that goal.

> We face new challenges at home and from international competitors, such as the Pacific Rim countries. They do not rely on market forces alone in education and neither should we. It is time now to get to the heart of raising standards – improving the quality of teaching and learning.

> (DfEE 1997a: 9, 11)

These quotations represent the narrative of past failure that runs through this part of the White Paper; there is an analysis of English educational provision that suggests that it is failing the average and below average pupil because it is too elitist and because comprehensive schooling produced uniformity and a belief that 'all had the same ability' (p. 11). These problems are associated with past practices, structures and doctrines, and lead me on to consideration of the *silences* regarding governance.

A major silence concerns resources. It is interesting that the Foreword, by the Secretary of State for Education, states that 'Resources are not the sole answer to delivering our objectives', and goes on to remind readers that the first budget of this government had provided additional resources for education. Towards the end of this first section there is a brief note to the effect that 'we recognise that effective support also requires investment; that is our deal with parents, pupils and teachers' (p. 13).

A further silence concerns the purposes of education, beyond the drive towards economic competitiveness. There is some discussion of agendas beyond the economic, but these appear to me to be rather muted and unspecific, particularly in comparison with the clarity of targets for improved literacy and numeracy, and general raising of standards. Here are these references: 'A good education provides access to this country's rich and diverse culture, to its history and to an understanding of its place in the world. It offers opportunities to gain insight into the best that has been thought and said and done' (p. 9). (Note the modernized reference to Arnold's definition of culture.) There is something oddly static and old-fashioned about this paragraph that makes it read like a necessary but rather empty gesture of reassurance. Then we have:

> There are wider goals of education which are also important. Schools, along with families, have a responsibility to ensure that children and young people learn respect for others and for themselves. They need to appreciate and understand the moral code on which civilised society is based and to appreciate the culture and background of others. They need to develop the strength of character and attitudes to life and work, such as responsibility, determination, care and generosity, which will enable them to become citizens of a successful democratic society.
>
> (DfEE 1997a: 10)

This seems to me to be a highly compressed version of the complex sets of aims for education that are usually organized around personal and social development, political capacity and citizenship. It is a set of propositions that brings together some ideas that are in uneasy juxtaposition; for example, *the* moral code and 'culture and background of others'. (Who are the 'others'?) It is also interesting that the concept of 'success' is attached to democracy, thereby placing the economic agenda alongside the social/political.

What ideas and categories are presented regarding social exclusion/inclusion?

There is very little in this section of the White Paper on exclusion/inclusion. The principle of including all children as achievers of educational success is evident, and is underlined by the setting out of targets for numeracy and literacy and for school improvement. I have looked at the rest of the document for this section because of the significance of the concepts exclusion/inclusion. The strongest relevant statement comes in the Secretary of State's Foreword, where he says: 'To overcome economic and social disadvantage and to make equality of opportunity a reality, we must strive to eliminate, and never excuse, under-achievement in the most deprived areas of the country' (p. 3).

This reference to economic and social disadvantage and deprivation is quite unusual in the document, and suggests that there are factors contributing to low attainment beyond the school. These are not discussed in any detail, but may be inferred from the sections on partnership with parents, who are constructed as having duties and obligations in relation to their children's learning, and a particular responsibility for discipline and attendance at school. There is a section on exclusions from school, which obviously connects to the larger questions of exclusion/inclusion with which we are concerned, but it is mainly concerned with reducing overall rates of exclusion (which have increased dramatically in recent years) and making appropriate provision for disaffected pupils. There is concern that exclusion contributes to low achievement among boys and to crime.

The final reference to the issue of exclusion/inclusion comes in the section of the White Paper on 'Modernizing the comprehensive principle'. The major principle of modernization is the abandonment of mixed ability teaching and the encouragement of diversity of provision, within and between schools.

> The demands of the future will require that everyone succeeds in secondary education. We are not going back to the days of the 11 plus; but neither are we prepared to stand still and defend the failings of across the board mixed ability teaching. The debate is sterile and provides no solutions. We intend to modernise comprehensive education to provide inclusive schooling which provides a broad, flexible and motivating education that recognises the different talents of all children and delivers excellence for everyone.
>
> (DfEE 1997a: 37–8)

This policy direction, and the establishment of foundation, community and aided schools, obviously has implications for inclusion/exclusion. These will need to be explored through further research; for example, on the operation of setting and on the operation of selection for or choice of the different types of school. We are, for the moment, confined to reading the text. My interpretation of it is that it is attempting to construct selective mechanisms within a framework that claims inclusivity. My reading is influenced by knowledge that lies outside the text; for example, in relation to the tendency of setting to produce and reproduce groups of dissaffected and failing pupils. There is also a strong tendency for diversity in English education to turn into hierarchy, and, of course, the historically based pattern of provision in different schools that carries forward into foundation and community schools cannot be ignored. Focusing more specifically on the text, the messages about inclusion and exclusion are about educational success and failure, with a strong theme of employability. There is very little invocation of alternative, and sometimes powerful, versions of exclusion/inclusion in relation to citizenship rights, entitlement, human development, self-realization, etc. Nor is there any discussion of a relationship between inclusion and exclusion, along the lines that we have already discussed; that is, a growth in inequalities associated with the nature of economic change and development that privilege the 'included' but immiserate those who are unable to benefit.

Summary

My purpose in this discussion was not to provide a full-scale reading of this text, but to illustrate how text analysis might be done. It will be evident that my reading is informed by my general approach to the issues of restructuring of education and other services, and by the social science/critical theory approach that I am engaged in. Other readings will be different; reading text demands interpretation and interpretation is shaped by Seddon's 'lacework of meanings'. Once again, the principles of choice apply, so that the basis of a reading is made evident, and the arguments for it are explained and defended. The text is (usually) a public document, and may be read – and interpreted – by others, who may challenge your reading. There is no doubt that the authors of this text would have little time for my reading of it.

Reading policy texts is, in my view, a rather underdeveloped research skill, and one that should be more widely used. Texts help to contribute to the formal policy narrative, and may contribute useful information about the source of policy, its assumed scope and its understanding of pattern. I think the White Paper demonstrates well the usefulness of these categories in any critical reading of policy. Reading and re-reading of texts, and groups of related texts, reveals the reiteration of phrases and key words that encapsulate policy makers' assumptions, while the tone also suggests what is felt about how things should happen. The tone of the White Paper, for example, is *dirigiste*, with little trace of hesitancy, possibility of dissent or opportunity for discussion. Things *will* happen, there will be, we will have, standards will rise. It is a tone that is very instructive in terms of understanding how the new Labour administration understands policy making. In relation to the project I am discussing here, it is a valuable source of information on the model of governance that lies behind policy. It is a highly centralist and managerialist model, in my view, and I believe the text offers further support for my reading of the overall policy trajectory outlined at the beginning of the book.

For our more immediate purposes, it is also instructive in relation to inclusion and exclusion, but, I would suggest, more by what it omits than what it says directly. The lack of attention to inequality and the substitution of underachievement for inequality are highly significant. Although this is not discussed or defended in any detail, but implicit in the tone and direction of the document, the solution to exclusion is greater educational success, leading to greater employability. Beneath that assumption must lie the belief that if the workforce is sufficiently skilled, then global capital will be attracted to the UK and so ensure economic success. If you accept this prescription, then it is perfectly possible to read the White Paper as a heroic and innovative policy text, reversing past policy in both its content and its form; making public commitments and accepting responsibility for system redesign to an unprecedented degree. It can be read as an attempt to break free of the habits and prescriptions of the past, to deny the effects of past patterns, to transform the culture of English education. Thus, it is not simply a policy text, but a text that seeks to establish the discursive frameworks that shape possibilities for policy.

What, then, does this particular research example tell us about doing research on education policy? First, it should be noted that this is a particularly complex investigation, because it is attempting to explore the following things:

- *The explanatory power of globalization.* Is globalization a useful concept, what do we mean by it, are its processes visible in the different countries in the project, is it better understood as a slogan that policy makers use to justify actions rather than a significant process of change? What are its consequences for education and how do we see and understand evidence of them?
- *The shifting nature of governance.* What do we mean by it and how do we establish changes related to globalization? If governance encompasses state–civil society relationships, what can we leave out of our enquiry? How do we assess the significance of changes in education governance? How do we ensure accurate comparison across systems?
- *The meaning of social exclusion and inclusion.* How do we understand these terms, and how do we relate them to the issues noted above? How would we demonstrate a relationship between increased exclusion and changed governance? How do we measure exclusion? How do we take account of qualitative as well as quantitative measures of exclusion/inclusion? How do we relate these to national contexts?

The complexity of these issues does not make the research impossible, but it increases the requirement for participants to set out clearly the basis on which they are selecting and interpreting evidence, including texts. The collaborative research process also requires – and stimulates – the discussion of knowledge production in different contexts, and leads to scrutiny of the intellectual resources that we bring to the table, which are themselves shaped by shifts and flows in the global exchange of knowledge. The production of research outputs is also shaped by the relationship of research and policy in different national contexts, while the existence of the European Union as a client produces effects on some of the processes of investigation and reporting, as I have already noted.

This research example, then, is not a template for other investigations. What it seeks to show is how the processes of research, and the informing projects of research on policy, influence the outcomes of research. In attempting to make this process more transparent, I am continuing my argument for openness in the discussion of research orientation, and in research choices, because of my belief that we cannot achieve transparency through the use of the apparatus of hygienic research, but that we can move towards better understanding (more reliable, more valid research exchanges) if we articulate the principles of choice in policy research.

On a less ambitious scale, I hope I have persuaded you of the potential of policy text analysis. This is a form of research on education policy that does not demand much material resource, and it can be applied to all kinds of policy texts, including school-based texts. Policy text production is now a major part of work in education, so that resources for such enquiry are available at all levels of the system. Looking for connections between texts at different levels is an instructive research form that offers the possibility of tracing policy trajectories or assessing the effects of discursive frameworks on different actors. Enquiry that is focused on text may go well beyond texts, as we have seen, but there is also scope for research on the volume of text, on the impact of text production on education work (for teachers, headteachers, LEA officers, governors and others) and on the changing styles of policy text production. The style of policy text may tell us about the relative influence of officials and politicians in policy making, if we study texts over a period of time when change in that relationship might be taking place. Using policy texts as a research resource is one of the most accessible forms of research on education policy, and is to be commended not just for its accessibility, but because close reading of policy texts helps to generate critical, informed and independent responses to policy. Reading and interpreting texts can be an act of engagement with policy, for the researcher and those with whom she or he works.

Exclusion and inclusion: some further investigations

I want to move now from the scrutiny of policy text as a research resource to some other investigative techniques. Once again, I do this through discussion of some of my own work, in this case on the EAZs that were established following the White Paper discussed above. The programme of EAZs was announced in the section on 'Modernising the comprehensive principle'. They were aimed at constructing partnerships between schools, business, community and voluntary groups in areas 'with a mix of underperforming schools and the highest levels of disadvantage' (DfEE 1997a: 39).

As part of a team of researchers based at Keele University, I was interested in exploring the changed relationships in educational governance that were intended and that actually developed in a small sample of EAZs. The design of the research proposal permitted enquiry into what we judged to be significant themes; for example, what the creation of the EAZs implied for the future governance of education, how public–private partnerships were understood by participants in them and the meaning and potential of 'third way' policy making. We set out to explore the impact of EAZs on existing mechanisms of educational governance, and to study the forms and processes of governance that they produced. We also set out to find out more about the nature, scale and scope of partnerships with private enterprise, the meaning of this involvement and its impact on LEAs. Finally, we were concerned to explore the ways in which new collaborative relationships between agencies actually developed as policy networks, and their impact on existing cultures. Of course, some of these areas of enquiry produced data and analyses of practical use to those involved in the EAZs, but the primary purpose of the research, reflected in its main themes, was to understand the model of educational governance implicit – and sometimes explicit – in the EAZ project, and assess its appropriateness, in the light of what we know about changing governance, to the task of challenging inequality.

The research design associated with these topics was one that combined documentary analysis of formal policy papers with interviews with participants in the schemes, representing all the interests involved. In the semi-structured interviews, i.e. interviews following a schedule of areas/headings to be explored, we sought to explore the intentions of the participants, the ways in which they read the structures of opportunity and constraint available through the initiative and the ways in which they conceptualized educational purposes and relationships. We also gathered data through observation of meetings, in which we were looking at the ways in which participants developed and pursued their interests.

The research resources here are varied. They include policy text analysis, interviewing and observation. All approaches generate a considerable amount of data. All the data require interpretation. Another issue for the research team was time – this was a major concern, as the EAZs were developing at such speed that there was always concern to be where things were happening, and a nagging sense of insecurity about making the wrong choices. The speed of the development also contributed to the difficulty of the research task in a different way, and that had to do with going into uncharted territory. No one involved in the policy project was completely clear about how it would work; possibilities were constantly altering in the early stages, and the rapidity of implementation by the DfEE meant that it was quite hard for the participants to imagine or articulate the future of their planned Zone in any detail. They had only really begun to address the issues that we wanted to discuss; in some cases we were bringing them issues that they had not yet thought about.

There were other problems; for example, the issue of access to these processes, particularly when delicate negotiations were under way with potential sponsors. The areas that we sought to explore inevitably raised questions about the appropriateness of business involvement in educational provision, and about the balance of power among the participants. In these circumstances we had to accept that certain discussions or papers remained confidential, and could not be quoted, or that some of our research outputs would be monitored. Such relationships could work productively, as they involve discussions about the interpretation of events with all of those involved, including the researchers. Returning to the issue of knowledge production, involvement in this situation also leaves the research team vulnerable to 'capture' by one or other of the interests represented in the Zone.

Despite these constraints and problems, the research remains possible, and valuable, in my view. Here are some of my reasons:

- As there was no pre-existing pattern for EAZs, we were able to explore their development as it happened, and to get close to the ways in which people made meaning from the policy.
- As the process involved so many of the interests and actors that are part of the cultural shift required in education, we were able to explore the impact of changed governance on these key groups.
- The EAZs represented new policy relationships, and we were able to see how these operated, where power lay and how it was created and enacted.
- The EAZs challenged our preconceptions as researchers; we were highly sceptical of business involvement and concerned about the impact on established patterns of provision and on established relationships. These preconceptions followed from our 'reading' of current policy, and had to take account of evidence of productive change in the areas we studied.

There are other points that may be briefly made here, and that may be of use in thinking about similar projects. In particular, it is interesting to consider how far the interview process in such a study can be connected to my earlier arguments for feminist methodology in creating an exchange, or a productive conversation, between people, one of whom is formally a researcher. I have already indicated that we were constrained from offering too much of our opinions where we knew they might alienate or irritate. But there was an element of shared experience of LEA administration, or of voluntary, community or union work, that provided a useful resource for exchange with interviewees. The need to ensure that we uncovered what people were thinking, at a stage when they might still be in the process of working it out, made us quite reliant on formal structured schedules, so that all of us covered the same ground and covered it thoroughly. And we had to be persistent in order to assist in the process of clarification of thinking that the research required; we had to be sure that we understood what was said.

I have discussed two projects that deal with education policy in relation to inclusion/exclusion. I have talked about some of the difficulties in research design and in the collection and analysis of data, with the intention of highlighting the problematic nature of interpretation. I have also continued to advocate my own preferred approach to those difficulties. There are, of course, other ways of proceeding, as we have seen in our discussion of theoretical resources for policy research, and the different ways in which they shape enquiry. Research on policy in progress is seen by some as offering a way of exploring policy as it happens, while considering its connection to broader agendas of change or continuity. No particular interpretation of these changes and continuities is overtly subscribed to, but the different ways in which they may be understood are noted. In the next section I offer some examples of this approach.

Researching policy in process

There are a number of examples of published research on policy in progress that provide interesting guidance on the kinds of research resources drawn on for such work. A very well known example is the work of Whitty *et al.* (1993) on the City Technology Colleges (CTCs), which used interviews with key architects of the CTC scheme to clarify its objectives, and then considered how they worked in practice, particularly in relation to key issues such as selection and sponsorship, as well as the project of injecting 'entrepreneurship' into English schooling. There are parallels between the CTC initiative and the EAZs; for instance, they are both quite small-scale in numbers, but carry a heavy weight of policy expectations in terms of transformation of the culture, and, especially, involvement of private enterprise. They could both be understood as policy responses to a process of economic transformation, yet they may also be read as reinstating old patterns of selection through vocationalized curricula. They also share the characteristics of speedy, and relatively unplanned, implementation.

In an article called 'Researching a policy in progress', Whitty *et al.* (1993) discuss their research design, which involved a mix of interviews with participants in the CTC project and observation of management, curriculum and pedagogy in the newly established CTCs. The research design included visits to other systems, notably the North American, to consider the impact on English policy of magnet schools. The research questions that emerged as the focus of the investigations were:

- What are the origins and purposes of CTCs?
- How has the policy changed during the course of investigation?
- How innovative are the CTCs?
- How dependent is their innovativeness on the nature of their funding and their organizational autonomy?
- What kinds of intakes are CTCs recruiting and how well do these match the criteria laid down by the DES?
- What effects are CTCs having on LEA provision and on other schools?

Note that the questions are said to have emerged as the focus for investigation; they are not established by the orientation of the researchers. The process of emergence is emphasized because, as the researchers point out, they needed to adapt their research design to the constantly changing policy context of the late 1980s, in which a number of major initiatives appeared simultaneously. In presenting detailed research evidence in their book, Whitty *et al.* (1993) produce detailed answers to these questions, and emphasize throughout that any conclusions they reach must be tentative because of the incompleteness of the process of policy implementation. They point out the contradictory nature of the evidence that they have, which suggests to them that they 'read' the policy in process as open to adaptation at the 'street level', and also that there is no clear economizing agenda at work in this policy, but a combination of traditional and innovative policy. The research provides a very clear model of reporting and discussion, with some connection to the broader questions of global economic change and postmodernity. It concludes with a balanced statement that reviews the extent to which CTCs may be understood as *New Schools for New Times*. It explores that issue under the following headings: Marketizing welfare? Depoliticizing education? A global movement? A facet of post-Fordism? A postmodern phenomenon? Reworking old themes? It brings the points made under these headings into a final section on continuity and change. They conclude:

> Despite the development of new forms of accumulation and changes in the state's mode of regulation, together with some limited changes in patterns of social and cultural differentiation in contemporary Britain, the continuities seem just as striking as the discontinuities.
>
> (Whitty *et al.* 1993: 180)

I have included this example of research using a variety of data-gathering methods – text, interviews and observation – because it offers high quality research reporting on major education policy issues. It is part of a continuing engagement with major policy issues that has resulted in work on the Assisted Places Scheme (Edwards *et al.* 1989) as well as the research described here. It provides a contrast with my own approach, which seeks a more explicit statement of perspective from the researcher, together with open discussion of choices. As Edwards *et al.* point out, I have criticized studies of this kind on the basis that they tend to provide rich descriptive data but to lack any significant reference to broader issues or to explicit theoretical perspectives . . . But research of apparently narrow empirical scope is not necessarily myopic or empiricist. Thus, while trying to make sense of a highly controversial and certainly complicated policy initiative, we have also been seeking to locate CTCs not only within the broader context of the Education Reform Act but also within an understanding of the changing modes of regulation that have been emerging within the economy, the state, and civil society.

(Edwards et al. 1989: 103)

This positioning, then, offers you an alternative to my theory-driven model.

Other researchers have taken the contradictory and conflicting evidence available from studies of policy in process as the basis for construction of a model of understanding policy that gives 'equal time' to policy formulation and policy implementation (though they regard these divisions as arbitrary). The intention is to get away from the problem of all-powerful policy delivered to recipients, but also to scrutinize the transmission and redesign of policy 'on the ground', so that it is not categorized as either inert acceptance or romantic resistance. Ball and Bowe, for example, repudiate state control models, and suggest that

> the policy process is a good deal more complex than this, and that there is a dialectical process in which the 'moments' of legislation (The Act), documentation (from the NCC, DES etc.) and 'implementation' (the work of teachers) may be more or less loosely-coupled.

(Bowe and Ball 1992: 98)

This enables us to understand policy as a cycle of processes in which practitioners are conceptualized as actively engaged with the process of policy making, in ways that may modify its forms and messages. The contradictory elements of CTC provision at school level, and some of the operations of the Technical and Vocational Education Initiative (TVEI), may be understood in these terms.

However, the recent growth in implementation studies has become less preoccupied with finding good social science explanations and more concerned with ensuring smooth policy delivery. There is a strong policy analysis orientation is this form of policy implementation study, as exemplified in the following quotation:

> The research highlights how limited the ability of individuals and groups at one system level can be to make policies on behalf of those at other levels which will cover all eventualities. It points to the need for strong cross-level monitoring strategies to be put in place by the major policy makers, so that cracks may be detected, and, hopefully, sealed up

before they develop into major gaps between policy intention and practice at sites of implementation.

(Wallace and Pocklington 1998: 8)

I have argued that as education research – especially education policy research – is a terrain of struggle in which the current policy context is a powerful influence, it is insufficient to think of methodology as concerned only with technical procedures and data-gathering processes. Methodologies are connected to the larger narratives already encountered in this book; they reflect choices that are based on orientation to policy research, and that in turn influences the topic and the resources brought to bear on the research problem. In the same way that education policy has been shaped by the policy context, so that context acts on the formation of research and the research community. We have discussed the ways in which the teacher–research relationship is being redesigned to reflect policy. In the apparently autonomous higher education institutions too, managerialism makes an impact on researchers' identities as autonomous knowledge producers. Marketized research relationships have produced a breakdown of trust, and diminished reciprocity; research communities are constituted as arenas of competition, mistrust, protection and manipulation of knowledge, bargaining and positioning.

To counteract these tendencies, I am arguing that the research community of academics and teachers should adopt the social field of education (policy) research as an arena of investigation, but in a reflexive mode that is conscious of the processes of knowledge production inherent in policy, and with attention to the personal dispositions that emerge in this competitive, fragmented milieu, and their consequences for the field of intellectual enquiry and those who labour in it. This could involve the cooperative development of an agenda for self-controlled research that focuses on the impact of changing material and social processes on research and teacher identities. It would require scrutiny from within the research community of the processes of knowledge production, including historically grounded work that sought to explore theoretical shifts in the various disciplines that sustain education research and shifts in policy–research relations.

In the next chapter I consider some of the advantages of a historically grounded approach to education policy research.

6 | History and education policy research

The importance of historical context

I have argued throughout this book that education policy making is to be defined and understood very broadly. Education policy is not confined, in my view, to the formal relationships and processes of government, nor only to schools and teachers, and to legislation affecting them. The broad definition requires that we understand it in its political, social and economic contexts, so that they also require study because of the ways in which they shape education policy. If we exclude them, we are not providing a comprehensive picture. We are also required, I believe, to explore the effects of prevailing ideologies on education policy.

One way of approaching this is to look at the history of education policy making and its accompanying narrative of explanation of education policy that is provided by policy research. I have already introduced this idea in my treatment of teachers as a perennial policy problem, subject to different kinds of historically framed solutions, and to interpretation of these events, which is itself produced in specific historical conditions. Clarification of the historical context within which education policy in England has emerged and continues to be framed illustrates the ways in which explanations of events are tied into prevailing ideologies and shaped by them (which in turn, of course, underlines the need to take account of ideologies in framing research practices; see the Tooley–Gewirtz and Ball debate above). It is interesting to consider how recent changes in education policy making have been dealt with by policy researchers. Since the early 1980s there has been a transformation of education policy making, in both content and process. There were early indications of change, but few predictions of its scope or impact. Most discussions of the transitional period from the late 1970s to the late 1980s stress how far policy then was departing from post-war conventions surrounding education policy making. These conventions included the following assumptions:

- that the aims of education policy were to improve access and equality of opportunity;
- that its processes were essentially consensual, reflecting the shared concerns of the three major policy-making groups, central government, local government and the teachers.

These conventions were understood to have been established by the 1944 Education Act, which was interpreted as having instituted a devolved system of educational administration, allowing considerable autonomy to schools and LEAs, and avoiding the concentration of policy-making powers at the centre. The then recent abuse of power over education in Nazi Germany engendered strong resistance to powerful ministerial controls. The architects of the 1944 Act saw it as offering the right to a role in policy to a balanced selection of legitimate interests. The maintenance of a balance of power between the teachers, the LEAs and the centre depended on a workable consensus about education policy, and that consensus was developed around principles of access and entitlement, regardless of background, and a belief in human capital theory. Ideas about entitlement were linked to post-war conceptions of citizenship and the development of a Keynesian welfare state as the model provider of essential services.

The 1944 Education Act was based on the assumption that these ideas about citizenship, entitlement and access to 'secondary education for all' were best delivered through a state-run partnership of the ministry/DES, LEAs and the teachers. Throughout the 1950s, 1960s and even the early 1970s, these central assumptions held, though they came under strain. The strengthening of equality of access into equality of opportunity challenged the tripartite division of technical, secondary modern and grammar schools provided for in the Act, and revealed divisions among the partners, especially over comprehensive reorganization. However, although the partnership was tested, it is understood to have survived until the 1970s. In this period education policy is generally understood as decentralized, consensual and involving teachers, LEAs and central government, with considerable autonomy remaining with schools and teachers. What I want to point up here is the extent to which explanations of policy, and research on policy, were permeated with assumptions about partnership; in particular, about its desirability and its prevalence. I am reiterating my point that research on policy making, and the construction of knowledge about policy, is itself shaped by assumptions that often reflect prevailing patterns of provision and the ideologies that sustain them. Consider how rapidly the partnership model become redundant. Explanations of policy that drew upon it were invalidated by the loss of partnership status of LEAs and teachers.

Historical explanations, like the concept of 'partnership', are themselves permeated with assumptions. They are not simple and straightforward factual accounts. Historical explanation is an exemplar of competing world views, and of rival ontological, epistemological and methodological assumptions. Looking at how the history of education policy has been written – and, in effect, examining the history of policy research – allows us to see the extent to which explanation and 'factual' account become intermingled. It also provides an introduction to the place of theory in research on policy. As Harold Silver puts it, in his plea for education policy to be studied as history and theory:

> Education since 1944, like any social process or institution in any period, raises difficult questions of description, and therefore of selection and emphasis. Whether historians remain committed to description and selection, or more explicitly to interpretation, their work is influenced or informed or governed by some kind of theory – from the least explicit, 'common sense' kind, to the most explicit and overtly ideological. Historical selection is not random, and is conducted within the terms of the historian's understandings of social, economic, political or otherwise defined processes. The very conceptions 'social', 'economic', 'political', 'cultural' and other categories involve commonly understood and accepted definitions and models – some of which we have previously seen emerging clearly only in the late 19th and early 20th centuries. Historical description and analysis are often conducted as an adjunct to case studies in the relevant theory – whether or not it is explicit. As generations of historians have learned and re-learned, to try to identify the history–theory relationship is to be involved in cross-frontier debates and disputes with sociologists, philosophers, and political and economic theorists. It also means involvement in profound controversies amongst historians themselves, and amongst variants of the same historical and theoretical standpoint.
>
> (Silver 1983: 240)

The history–sociology relationship is potentially a very rewarding one in education policy research, but perhaps not fully exploited. Much of the history of education is unreflexive and atheoretical, and signally fails to illuminate the impact of the past on the present or the effect of historically constructed frameworks for research on current enquiry. There are exceptions to this general rule, of course. Richard Johnson's work illuminates the enduring patterns and preoccupations of provision in England. In particular, he explores the ways in which those patterns permeate the workings of policy in the current context:

> It is often argued, especially by those who say this is a good thing, that English education is peculiarly 'decentralised'. In a sense this is (or was) true, but it might be more revealing to say that it has been heavily localised. A succession of social groups and alliances have acquired an

important stake in local educational organisation, from the eighteenth-and nineteenth-century clergy and gentry, the Dissenting churches, the committees of urban middle class subscribers, the municipal alliances of the school board era, the socialist local authorities of the early twentieth century, and the suburban state professionals of the post-war period.

Yet this formation – 'the educational interest' or 'educational establishment', if you will – is itself quite a restricted public based on exclusive forms of knowledge, social interest and expertise. As Mr Baker and his colleagues understand very well, there are major limits to the political reach of the expert educational public. Local involvement has always co-existed with considerable powers of central intervention and control. Not weakness of the centre but a central–local balance of power has been the pattern. Local participation has always been vulnerable to legislative innovations and administrative adjustments from Westminster and Whitehall. Under favourable conditions, governments, in alliance with central administrators, can change the rules of the game altogether, outflanking local opposition. The spectacular routing of local authorities in the Baker Act, and the abolition of the Greater London Council and the Inner London Education Authority (ILEA) are not so unprecedented here. We might list the Revised Code, the abolition of school boards, and the inter-war financial cuts, as equivalent instances.

(Johnson 1989: 99–100)

These insights make a powerful resource for 'reading' recent policy on governance, modernizing the comprehensive principle and economizing education.

History as progress

One of the problems that needs to be tackled by those attracted to historically based policy research is the conscious and unconscious construction of history as the story of progress. As we have seen, this is a particular characteristic of work on the post-war years, in the period around and following the 1944 Education Act. Silver offers a trenchant criticism of research that emphasizes the construction of better futures through welfare state planning, that falls into the dangers of 'idealism and error or of excessive confidence and over-simplification'. He goes on to explore the ways in which those ideas shaped research and also seemed to produce clear guidance for policy and action:

How and why these forms of confidence, that sense of choice, the apparent possibility of action were diminished . . . are widespread international questions . . . A sensitive dialogue between the historical evaluation of experience and the intrusive nature of theory, has never been more necessary. Without it, the dangers are now either those of unproductive frustration, or the denial or romanticization of the past, limited gains, and the abandonment of policy to rhetoricians.

(Silver 1983: 241)

Silver's warning follows from the fact that much education policy history has been written as the history of progress, in which the development of the system is charted as a kind of natural growth. From the first grant-in-aid in 1833, to the establishment of a central department in 1856, through the various Acts of the nineteenth and twentieth centuries, education policy reflects the growth of state responsibility for provision, according to this narrative of progress. Researchers on the history of policy rarely discuss the reasons for that progress, because it is seen as inevitable that the state recognizes education as necessary to the general good. Yet the contested development of state provision, and the struggles about content, access and quality that it encapsulated, do much to explain tensions in the pattern of current provision. Some researchers consider that a major reason for the low status of vocational education, and the elitist nature of academic provision, is the late acceptance by the English state of responsibility for mass provision (Green 1989), and we have already seen how Johnson traces the continuing influence of historical patterns of provision and relationships among providers.

The view of the growth of state provision as natural contributed to the version of policy-making that dominated research from the 1940s to the 1980s. In that account, teachers, parents, LEAs and central government – the major interests – were understood to *negotiate* education policy, not without difference, but in broad agreement.

An example: the 1944 Education Act

The 1944 Education Act represents the apogee of welfare state provision. It gave access to secondary education 'for all'. It was imbued with the rhetoric of entitlement and citizenship. That rhetoric was not unimportant, but the 1944 Act also had practical significance for working-class children, in that it provided genuine secondary (rather than extended elementary) education throughout the country, free of charge.

This looks like a departure from the pattern of differentiation. Indeed, the 1944 Act has been seen as a final victory after a prolonged struggle by the working class for secondary education, a victory over the effects of policies from the 1870s to the 1930s which had reasserted the elementary–secondary division and confined working-class education to elementary schools. Such an interpretation underplays the limits of the 1944 Act, in which, as the Centre for Contemporary Cultural Studies (CCCS) (1987) points out, egalitarian rhetoric was not matched by the structure of provision. The 1944 Act provided not for a uniform system of secondary education but for a tri-partite one, which, for all the talk of 'parity of esteem', reflected divisions of class and subject status.

The threefold division of grammar, secondary modern and technical schooling had its roots in the hierarchy of values of Victorian adminis-trators, founded in their turn on the Aristotelian/Platonic philosophy they studied in public schools. That background, and those assumptions, perme-ated English education and had significant consequences for policy. Bishop, in his study of the growth of a central authority in English education (the transformation of the Board of Education into the Ministry and thence the DES), explains that:

> The rise of a central authority for English education has been a slow, tortuous, makeshift, muddled, unplanned, disjointed and ignoble pro-cess. By its very nature the form that authority assumed was bound to be a reflection of the social structure and educational philosophy of the age in which it evolved. But then, in the course of time, the authority itself helped to reinforce that structure and perpetuate that philosophy. Unconsciously at first, and later, perhaps, with deliberate intent, the architects of the English educational system proceeded to construct it along the lines of the Platonic model described in *The Republic*. The children of gold, silver and iron were given the education deemed appropriate to their supposed abilities and the state's requirements. This separate development found expression not only in the schools but in the institutions of central government . . . Herein lay one of the prin-cipal legacies that administrators and politicians of the Victorian era bequeathed to their successors; for the three-fold division of the central authority which characterised the latter half of the nineteenth century supplied the blue-print, if not the rationale, for the tripartite division of secondary education which characterised the greater part of the twen-tieth.
>
> (Bishop 1971: 276)

These divisions were clearly reflected in the 1944 Act, and their importance was confirmed by the officials who helped to construct that Act and shape provision after the war. These officials took active, if often covert, steps to discourage the multilateral (comprehensive) schools which some LEAs wanted to institute. They instead encouraged adherence to the tripartite div-ision of grammar, secondary modern and secondary technical schools stipu-lated in the Act, using technical arguments to support the preservation of the grammar–secondary modern division in particular (see CCCS 1987; Gewirtz and Ozga 1990).

There is, then, at least in this historical interpretation, a way of telling the 'story' of education policy making from the 1860s to the 1940s which emphasizes certain points:

1 Policy makers' preoccupation with differentiation, i.e. the provision of different types of education for different social classes.
2 The maintenance of differentiation through market-led/*laissez-faire* ideologies which encouraged the continued existence of multiple providers (church charities, etc.) but which also fostered (indeed required) strong regulatory state activity in the social and political spheres.
3 The tension created by attempts to redefine the boundaries of schooling or abolish them altogether – in the nineteenth century the pressure to extend elementary education, in the twentieth century (and especially after 1944) the pressure for comprehensive education.
4 The restricted range of options available for the management of this tension, and the shifts between centralized control and decentralization depending on the social, economic and political context.

It is interesting to consider these key points in a critical narrative of the history of provision in England from the perspective of the 1990s, and to return to concepts of pattern and its enduring effect on provision. This is a reading that emphasizes the long endurance of institutional patterns and assumptions, and the consequent need for sustained activity if policy change is desired.

However, the conventional narratives of the 1944 Act are much less critical and more heroic in tone. For example:

> There was a groundswell of social and political opinion that there could be no returning to the social order of the 1930s: idleness, poverty, disease, ignorance and squalor had to give way to employment, income, personal dignity, health and opportunity. The unity which had won the war would recreate a new more just, open and modern society. While Keynes offered the design for economic support, Butler provided the framework for educational opportunity and the possibility of social mobility that could dissolve a rigid, outmoded, class-divided society:

> The state came to be seen as something vaster and more beneficent . . . as the real guarantor of reform and reconstruction . . .
>
> (Middlemas 1979)

> This post-war partnership, though contracted, had widespread political appeal and formed a cross-party consensus for a generation. A state, a system of rule, had been constituted which endured. Its organising of power and task were legitimated by a moral and political order whose primary value was justice as fairness: the foundation stone of common citizenship.
>
> (Ranson 1990: 3–5)

As you would expect, I argue that a number of qualifications of this view of the 1944 Act as the embodiment of justice, defined as fairness, need to be noted. It was Butler's intention to frame a much stronger, more centrist Act. He was prevented from doing so because of concern among his own back-benchers about excessive central control over education, a concern given particular force by the wartime context, and because of the need for pro-longed and delicate negotiations with the churches. Yet some of the centrist character remained, notably the 'control and direction' powers invested in the Secretary of State and the 'duties' laid on LEAs. There is clear evidence of officials' largely successful attempts to 'manage' the pattern of policy for secondary provision (Gewirtz and Ozga 1990). That they did not altogether succeed was a consequence of the situation created by wartime, by bombed schools, by the chaos of evacuation and by the scarce resources available to the fledgling Ministry to oversee the creation of a secondary education system. Teachers and LEAs had scope to influence provision and to assert themselves as partners to an extent which acted as a counterbalance to the minister's 'control and direction'.

While a very important factor in establishing the idea of partnership was the post-war political context and the prevalence of ideas of entitlement – justice as fairness – which fuelled the creation of the welfare state, it was not an idea that was uncontested. It is at this point that we need to be reminded, again, of the problematic nature of state policy. As has been pointed out above, the welfare state solution followed from increased recognition of entitlement, from the state's need to deal with problems in the political and social spheres, particularly the raising of post-war expectations. The limits to such a solution, i.e. its inevitable collision with economic and regulatory demands, should also be apparent, as should the tendency for welfare states to reinforce demands based on entitlement: this is Offe's (1985) argument that welfare states ultimately cease to be a solution and instead become a part of the problem.

I have attempted to introduce a degree of complexity into an understanding of the 1944 Act as a piece of policy. My intention is that you see that Act as operating simultaneously and as part of a continuous and shifting historical process which produces different solutions to continuing problems, solutions that depend, in part, on which problem is defined as most urgently requiring solution.

Elites in policy

I want to discuss another example of historical research in education policy making, which connects to the discussion above. In the account of the 1944 Act (above), I argue that officials attempted to maintain the principle of differentiation that Johnson suggests forms the cornerstone of English provision. My reasons for advancing this argument against the conventional imagery of the 1944 Act as reformist are based on research that carries forward the ideas in the Bishop quotation about the influence of Plato on the elite group of officials at central and local level who exerted considerable influence on education policy. I review some of the content of that research now, in order to explore its usefulness as a contrast with pluralistic treatments of the 1944 Act as the cornerstone of partnership.

The research project on which this argument is based was carried out with Sharon Gewirtz and re-examined the concept of partnership in the post-war period. The project, in fact, has a number of aims. At a relatively straightforward level it is concerned to discover more about post-war education policy making, as the range of writing on the period is quite narrow, both Gosden's administrative histories (Gosden 1976; Gosden and Sharp 1978) and Lowe's social history (Lowe 1988) being firmly located within a pluralist perspective. In addition, we wanted to address the difficulty of bringing together an explicit theoretical framework on elites and their role in policy making with empirical research which could, to a degree, speak for itself, and thus avoid the charges levelled by Silver against the CCCS of using history 'like the captions on archaeological exhibits – produced as shorthand guides to an already established collection' (Silver 1983: 251).

To this end, we examined a number of archive sources in the Public Record Office, the Association of Education Committees' archive in Leeds, Lady Shena Simon's collection in Manchester and the National Union of Teachers' archive, and we also carried out a number of extended, unstructured interviews with key figures from the period, in particular with former directors of education. We wanted to explore the impact on policy making in this period of figures who remain in place while politicians come and go. We also felt that too much attention had been paid to politicians rather than officials in the study of education policy making, as a result of pluralist concentration on government and party interest or interest group politics. In the words of one HMI, Matthew Arnold, 'He who administers, governs, because he infixes his own mark and stamps his own character on all public affairs as they pass through his hands.'

Certainly, nineteenth- and twentieth-century officials such as Lingen, Morant and Selby-Bigge would have endorsed this view. Lingen, for example, appearing before a Commission of Inquiry concerned about the growth of official control, remarked that he had 'yet to learn that the government is not in the hands of the permanent officials'. Despite the denials of official control or dominance of policy making by former civil servants, like Toby Weaver (1979) and others, it is hard to believe that the influence of officials was as minimal as they claim. Indeed, Stewart Ranson has found evidence of it even in the most unpromising, and more recent, circumstances (Ranson 1985). The effects of the continuity of views, backgrounds and assumptions that run through the Board of Education to the Ministry and then to the Department have yet to be fully explored.

The educational background of the Board/Ministry officials is even more restricted than that of the rest of the Civil Service. Gail Savage, researching the educational background of Board officials between 1919 and 1939 (179 men), found that 60 per cent were Oxbridge, but that senior posts went to Oxford, not Cambridge graduates (Savage 1983). Virtually every man who held one of the top three ranks at the Board had been to Oxford (usually Balliol) and one of the Clarendon schools (usually Winchester or Wellington). This, then, is the elite of an elite, and the predominance of Oxford is reflected in the group of able and ambitious men who entered educational administration in order to seize the opportunities offered by the 1944 Act. It is interesting to remember Tawney's (1938: 157) observation that:

> The capital fact about English education policy is that hitherto it has been made, except at brief intervals, by men, few, if any of whom have attended the schools principally affected by it, or would dream of allowing their children to attend them.

Further evidence of the survival of classical conditioning and of the policy making work of officials can be found in R. S. Wood's memo of 1946 to John Maud. These departmental memoranda offer a superb resource for researchers, as they document thinking and carry communications between officials and politicians in the days before technological advance made these exchanges invisible. Wood was Deputy Secretary at the Ministry, and had been Assistant Principal Secretary to the Board; Maud was the Permanent Secretary; the (Labour) Minister at this point was Ellen Wilkinson, who wrote on the memo, 'this is so good I would like a copy for my own use'. It is a sophisticated policy text, positioning a radical, reforming Minister carefully in relation to the prospect of major reform that officials did not want, but could not resist overtly:

> The Minister is very rightly pushing us to examine fundamentals – a very healthy, though painful, occupation for the Department. It is, of course, so much easier to keep a machine going – taking its purpose, process and production for granted – than to face up to the question – what are we doing with it after all?

> I do not criticise the Department unduly on this score. We are in the early stages of a transformation – from being a Department concerned to superintend others framing and running a public service of education, to becoming a Department charged to promote the education of the people and the execution of a national policy. We are, in short, passing from the role of critic to that of constructor. The framing of national policy must ultimately rest at the centre.

The memo also gives a clear indication of the views held by senior Departmental officials about the democratically elected local authorities. Wood had a clear view of partnership, and the appropriate balance of power within it:

> the truth is that however much LEAs and others of our partners may have felt it proper . . . to appear jealous of their rights and powers, and to object to any direction from Whitehall, there is little doubt that underneath there is a strong desire to be given a lead and a greater readiness to accept that lead.

Wood is an important figure in the shaping of the attitude of the people who operated the machinery of educational governance to the prospect of substantial change, and he helped to construct their strategic response to it, which seems to have consisted of public endorsement and private resistance. Wood had warned Holmes, the then Permanent Secretary, that they could not hold out indefinitely against reform, or a 'post-war labour government with a large majority will reject our advice entirely and seek guidance elsewhere'. To avoid this, the officials accepted free secondary education, but they successfully delayed the Act until they had ensured that the Norwood Commission would report in favour of the Platonic division, which they were then able to maintain as Ministry policy, defeating multilateralism (Simon 1986: 39). Indeed, as McCulloch points out, it is interesting to note how Norwood's proposals for curriculum reform were ignored, and his ideas of 'three kinds of mind' reduced to support for tripartitism (McCulloch 1988).

This material provides interesting evidence about the continuity of the official view and the methods by which officials made policy. I have drawn on evidence of the influence of permanent Ministry officials, and of co-operation – even collusion – between officials. It is interesting to consider whether this group formed, in effect, an elite within the policy-making apparatus of the state, both centrally and locally, that operated in pursuit of its own interests. I have already noted the restricted educational (and social) background of Board and Ministry officials. The Oxford bias among educational administrators remained remarkable throughout this period. Many outstanding administrators belonged to an informal group called the 'Young Contemporaries'; these included Toby Weaver and Norman Fisher. The All Souls Group, founded during the war by the Warden of All Souls, and John Newsom, with the intention of contributing to the discussions leading to the 1944 Act, was a further informal grouping of education officers, civil servants and headteachers. It included many well known directors, among them Ernest Salter Davies, Ernest Woodhead, Henry Morris, Douglas Cooke, Norman Fisher and Anthony Chenevix-Trench, and senior officials, including John Maud, Derek Morrell and Toby Weaver. Jack Longland, former Director of Education for Derbyshire, described the group's activities:

We used to meet in Oxford about once in every two or three months, and . . . we produced a sort of Green Paper of our own on what we thought the Butler Act ought to contain and in fact most of what we said was included in the Butler Act . . . The group still meets, I don't know whether it has any particularly useful function now, it probably has . . . I haven't been for some time but at that stage it was a ginger group of a quite interesting kind, not political, though of course it tended to face political issues, but with quite a lot of influence, and particularly through John Newsom and another member, John Maud, Lord Redcliffe-Maud later on, who became Permanent Secretary of the Department of Education and he was a very early member. And we always had two or three of the most intelligent senior civil servants from the Department of Education gladly coming to the All Souls Group and we all used to discuss what ought to be done next. It was totally unofficial.

(Interview September 1988)

The point of exploring these connections is to make some of the informal basis for policy making in education rather more visible: it is important to realize that the construction of the post-war system – and the 'partnership' mode of operating it – was carried out by a group with strong educational and social cohesiveness, and with a history of contact and easy communication. (For example, Maud was Newsom's tutor at Oxford, and continued to keep an open line to Newsom when he was Director of Education for Hertfordshire and Maud was Permanent Secretary) (McLure 1985: 50). The material presented here calls into question the existence of any significant degree of conflict between centre and locality, and distinguishes between the public appearance of negotiation over policy making, between different interests, and the private processes of administrative control.

In concluding this discussion of historical enquiry as a resource for research in education policy, I want to write some more about the issues raised by interviewing participants in policy making who have a 'formal' identity as policy makers.

Interviewing policy makers

The work that Sharon Gewirtz and I did on the Elites project on policy making, which is drawn on in the preceding section, led us to think about some more general issues in understanding policy through enquiry into the lives of policy makers (Ozga 1987; Ozga and Gewirtz 1994). Our main focus in the Elites project had been on the permanent officials in both central and local government of education. Our interest in the abiding continuities of English provision led us to this focus. Theoretically, we were interested in exploring the nature of the state administration within the state apparatus, following Poulantzas's arguments on the critical role of bureau-cratic organization in maintaining the dominant ideology (Poulantzas 1976). These ideas in turn connected to ideas about the class nature and composition of state bureaucracy and the ways in which it used knowledge and the production of knowledge as a way of maintaining unequal power relations.

That orientation towards the task required us to find out about the back-grounds of officials, their shared assumptions about the world, their for-mative experiences, their social relations and concepts of identity. From an original methodology that depended on long interviews on particular themes, we moved towards using life history approaches to these policy makers, in order to capture the content that we needed. We were unable to develop a full-scale life history approach, because of the constraints of time, but worked, instead, with Bertaux's notion of 'representativeness' (Bertaux 1981). Through this approach a small 'sample' is researched very thoroughly, until the researcher is satisfied that a 'representative' account of life and work has been achieved.

Life history work is challenging, and the position of the researcher in such an intimate and extended enquiry may be ambiguous. It is intrusive, as it seeks a full account without removal of the private from the public sphere. Intrusiveness may, perhaps, be justified when researchers argue that they are giving a voice to the dispossessed and disadvantaged, but the case is not easily made in these terms for elite groups of privileged actors. However, there are well made arguments (see, for example, Ferraroti 1990) for using life history work more generally because of its capacity to interrogate the space between structures and agency with which so much of this text has been preoccupied. There has been a considerable increase in interest in life history work on and by teachers, and such work is particularly illuminating if it spans the major recent changes in the nature of teachers' work, lives and careers (see, for example, Ball and Goodson 1985; Sikes 1997).

There are methodological issues that arise in the use of life history work. In my own work I have used this approach within a project that is also draw-ing on historical enquiry of more conventional kinds, as indicated above. That use of alternative sources is particularly useful when one is working with people who are being asked to recollect events after a considerable period has elapsed, for obvious reasons. It is also necessary to work, where possible, with alternative sources, because of the skill and experience of this particular group in self-presentation. The officials that I interviewed were all capable, active and engaged with education, even in retirement, and were very aware of their place in the narrative that they constructed.

This difficulty, of being drawn into the role of audience to an experienced policy maker, is compounded by the social relations that surround life his-tory work. The nature of the interviews demands quiet space and time, and this often means that the research is done in the informants' homes. In such a situation the researcher may become a guest, treated with courtesy, and offered hospitality. Others have commented on their unease in being caught by this situation:

> our approach has a number of implications. First and foremost, people have helped and trusted us, and this has influenced all our decisions in the presentation of evidence . . . In a sense our research was tapping the trust which binds members of the policy community across dispersed structural locations and even across lines of conflict on particular issues . . . If trust and help took us into the policy community, were we also 'taken in' in other ways? Was it gullibility that rendered us harmless?
>
> (McPherson and Raab 1988: 62)

On the other hand, there is a need to capture exactly that quality of management of a situation, and appropriate self-presentation, that lies at the heart of official power in policy making (or, more accurately, that used to, before the rise of political influence and the decline of official power). The self-conscious self-presentation of the 'public servant' was exactly what we wanted to capture for the project, so that there was no need to fracture that polished surface, or disrupt the narrative offered to us.

What was necessary was to be thoroughly prepared, and to accept that the 'interview' was likely to be controlled by the interviewee. Forms of control related to the structure of the account that was presented, as the interest in the 'life' allowed the interviewee to select moments and issues that were of most significance. Very often these accounts were punctuated with questions to the interviewer, sometimes checking on the level of preparation and knowledge of a topic, sometimes entering into a discussion of a particular event or idea. So there is a return to the idea of reciprocity discussed earlier in the discussion of feminist methodology, but without the same notion of equality between researcher and interviewee. Indeed, the need to enact the role of attentive audience to the 'public servant' could make considerable demands.

All these points serve to illustrate some of the difficulties encountered in using extended interviews or life history methods in working with policy makers who hold formal positions of authority and power. These problems may be compounded by the negotiation of access, in which the self-presentation of the researcher may become an issue. Historical work on distant policy events is much more accessible to these methods than current policy making, although, as we have seen, there are studies of current and recent policy that incorporate policy makers' accounts.

Stephen Ball has done work in this area, and written about its resources and constraints (Ball 1990, 1994). He takes a rather different approach from the one set out above, as he sees such work as combining ethnography, theories of the state and contradictions within the state deriving from

Althusser, and Foucauldian analysis of discourse as embodying power and producing power relations through the promotion of certain subjectivities and meaning systems over others. He explains further:

> In relation to these interpretational sources, my primary methodological point then is that, as data, the actors' 'voices' elicited in the fieldwork for the study can be interpreted in at least three different ways – the data is polyvocal.
>
> First, as 'real stories'; as accounts of what happened, who said what, whose voices were important. What is of interest here are descriptions of events, the account of character and key figures, moments and debates 'inside' policy. This is the 'how' of policy, the practicalities.
>
> Second, as discourse, as ways of talking about and conceptualising policy . . . The assertions, judgements, axioms and interpretations of actors are central here . . .
>
> Third, as interest representation (but not in any simple pluralist sense). This is data as indicative of structural and relational constraints and influences which play in and upon policy-making.
>
> (Ball 1994: 108–9)

Here we see an example of the resources for research on policy making being set out in some detail, before they are applied to the understanding of contemporary history that is derived from extended interviews with policy makers.

In conclusion, I would like to argue, as I did for policy text analysis, that the field would benefit from more work on policy making that uses extended or life history methods, or even oral history and biographical or autobiographical accounts. In particular, there is a need for the gathering of such data from educational workers who have lived through periods of transition, and whose experiences would provide a source for the better understanding of the experience of change in education. The gathering of such experience for teachers is an important act of collective memory, and helps in the project of enabling solidarity through the appropriate celebration of professional service and expertise, which is currently denied. It also has the potential to contribute fundamentally to the understanding of education policy, through its documentation and analysis of the 'voices' of some of the major 'actors' in the system.

7 | Conclusions: contesting the future?

This book has attempted to do a number of things. It has reviewed and discussed ways of approaching policy research in education, and has considered the impact of the changing policy context on how such research might be done, and on how research topics, problems and issues might be defined in such a context. In considering the content of policy research in education, the book has dealt with a number of diverse topics, but has attempted throughout that treatment to sustain a coherent argument about the value-orientation of research, about the need for theory in doing education policy research and about the need for explicitness in making research choices as the best means of achieving constructive conversations between researchers.

Running through these different issues is a further argument about the need for commitment to critical theory as a guide to and resource for research on education policy. Again, this argument is placed in context: the political/policy context that seeks to circumscribe the resources available to researchers and teachers with which they may think about their work and the nature and purposes of education, and the context of wider global change and its associated theoretical developments that challenge critical theory's hopes for rational improvement.

This book, then, is written against the grain of policy for education generally and for educational research in particular. It also goes against the flow of some social science theorizing which suggests that the critical theory project is a naive remnant of discredited modernity. It is, as Kenway has written, very difficult in these times in education to make 'hope practical' (Kenway *et al.* 1994). I feel obliged to make these arguments at this time because of the extent to which it seems to me that research on policy has been redefined as research for policy. There is now comprehensive policy activity on so many fronts that it looks set to produce highly controlled research practices, where topics, problems and resources will be established and regulated by policy makers, and spaces for independent research are diminished.

The diminishing of these spaces seems to me to be something that is happening to us, as researchers, as well as to material and practical resources. The creation of an orthodoxy of research practice, and the intolerance of powerful policy analysts/research consumers of dissent, or even of complexity, drives researchers into uneasy compromise, or acquiescence. The disciplinary mechanisms of the market operate on us and within us, and inhibit direct, critical response, because there are so many other people who depend on us for continued employment, and if we put ourselves 'outside' the policy-research networks, what impact will that have on them? And our institutional loyalties tie us to successful 'performance' against indicators that may themselves homogenize our research practice.

With some exceptions, the current policy of assaulting educational research has met with surprisingly little resistance, either from the research community or from the teaching profession. I have discussed some of the factors that I think contribute to that, in particular the absence of the capacity to suggest alternative indicators of validity of research to critics who try to import positivistic assumptions into territory where that language is not spoken. I have also written about the ways in which constructive conversations – competence in communication, including Habermasian notions of authenticity – have been inhibited by rather fierce and incoherent or obscure exchanges in the field. My support for articulation of principles of choice in policy research stems from hope that such explicitness would enable communication, and that it would also encourage closer engagement with social science theory among educational researchers, who would then be able to work across the boundaries of the discipline and gain support from other active (and less defensive) arenas of social policy.

At the same time, and as a matter of urgency, it is important that the research community engaged in education policy research finds ways of working with the teaching profession to support and sustain teachers in their struggles to retain authenticity in their work. One starting point for this is to recognize the commonality of our experience in the face of regulation, disciplinary practice, internal and external competition and denial of expertise. We may also wish to concede some commonality of response, rather than maintaining stereotypes that set us apart. Thinking about these shared experiences should also alert us to differences, and to the very significant role that the capacity to engage in research continues to play, even now, in providing alternatives to the hollowed out rhetoric of policy.

This returns me to my starting point, and the arguments at the beginning of the book that stressed the significance of education as a site for the development of capacity for social practice, and thus the continued significance of teachers, and also the remaining potential for contestation of 'post-Fordist pedagogy'. Critical research on policy assists in the uncovering of these possibilities, and critical policy researchers can assist the profession by insisting on complexity, resisting homogeneity, and recovering 'lost' histories.

Forms of contestation are not easy to define, but there are possibilities, and there are considerable resources within the critical research traditions discussed in this book. I conclude with Bourdieu's call for new forms of response to 'the myths of our time', where he writes that the new 'revolutionary conservative form of politics' requires:

> new forms of organisation of the work of contestation and of the organisation of contestation, of the task of activism. Our dream, as social scientists, might be for part of our research to be useful to the social movement . . . we would like to invent new forms of expression that would make it possible to communicate the most advanced findings of research. But that also presupposes a change of language and outlook on the part of researchers.
>
> (Bourdieu 1998: 58)

References

Abrams, P. (1982) *Historical Sociology*. London: Open Books.

Angus, L. (1993) Democratic participation or efficient site-management: the social and political location of the self-managing school, in J. Smyth (ed.) *A Socially Critical View of the Self-managing School*. London: Falmer Press.

Apple, M. (1989) *Official Knowledge*. London: Routledge.

Apple, M. (1993) *Official Knowledge: Democratic Education in a Conservative Age*. New York: Routledge.

Ball, S. (1990) *Politics and Policy-making in Education*. London: Routledge.

Ball, S. (1993) What is policy? Texts, trajectories and tool boxes, *Discourse*, 13(2): 10–17.

Ball, S. (1994) *Education Reform: A Critical and Post-structural Approach*. Buckingham: Open University Press.

Ball, S. (1997) Policy, sociology and critical social research: a personal review of recent education policy and policy research, *British Educational Research Journal*, 18: 5–14.

Ball, S. and Gewirtz, S. (1997) Is research possible? A response to Tooley, *British Journal of the Sociology of Education*, 18(4): 575–87.

Ball, S. and Goodson, I. (eds) (1985) *Teachers' Lives and Careers*. London: Falmer Press.

Barber, M. (1997) The Greenwich Lecture, Greenwich, September.

Bassey, M. (1998) Fuzzy generalisations and professional discourse, BERA Internet Conference, Paper F, March.

Bertaux, D. (ed.) (1981) *Biography and Society*. Beverly Hills: Sage.

Bishop, A. S. (1971) *The Rise of a Central Authority in English Education*. London: Macmillan.

Blackmore, J. (1995) Policy as dialogue, *Gender and Education*, 17(3): 27–34.

Bottery, M. (1995) Professionalism: a comparative study. Paper presented to European Conference on Educational Research, University of Bath, 14–17 September.

Bourdieu, P. (1992) *Language and Symbolic Power*. Cambridge: Polity Press.

Bourdieu, P. (1993) *Sociology in Question*. London: Sage.

Bourdieu, P. (1998) *Acts of Resistance*. Cambridge: Polity Press.

Bowe, R. and Ball, S. with Gold, A. (1992) *Reforming Education and Changing Schools*. London: Routledge.

Bradach, J. L. and Eccles, R. G. (1991) Price, authority and trust, in G. Thompson, J. Evans, R. Levačić and J. Mitchell (eds) *Markets, Hierarchies and Networks*. London: Sage.

Briault, E. (1976) A distributed system of educational administration, *Educational Administration*, 3(2): 55–63.

Brown, S., Duffield, W. and Riddell, S. (1995) School effectiveness research: the policy-makers' tool for school improvement?, *European Research Association Bulletin*, 2.

Caldwell, B. (1997) The impact of self-management and self-government on professional cultures of teaching, in A. Hargreaves and R. Evans (eds) *Beyond Educational Reform: Bringing Teachers Back In*. Buckingham: Open University Press.

Campbell, J. and Neill, S. J. (1994) *Primary Teachers at Work*. London: Routledge.

Carr, W. and Kemmis, S. (1986) *Becoming Critical: Education, Knowledge and Action Research*. Geelong: Deakin University Press.

Casey, K. (1995) *Work, Self and Identity after Industrialism*. London: Routledge.

Castells, M. (1996) *The Information Age: Economy, Society and Culture. Volume 1: The Rise of the Network Society*. Oxford: Blackwell.

Castells, M. (1997) *The Information Age: Economy, Society and Culture. Volume 2: The Power of Identity*. Oxford: Blackwell.

Castells, M. (1998) *The Information Age: Economy, Society and Culture. Volume 3: End of Millennium*. Oxford: Blackwell.

CCCS (1987) *Unpopular Education: Schooling and Social Democracy in England Since 1944*. London: Hutchinson.

Centre for Contemporary Cultural Studies (1991) *Unpopular Education: Schooling and Social Democracy in Education since 1944*. London: Hutchinson.

Clarke, J. and Newman, J. (1997) *The Managerial State*. Cambridge: Polity Press.

Commission on Excellence in Education (1998) *A Nation at Risk*. New York: State Department.

Connell, R. W. (1983) *Which Way Is Up? Essays on Sex, Class and Culture*. Sydney: Allen and Unwin.

Connell, R. W. (1986) *Teachers' Work*. Sydney: Allen and Unwin.

Connell, R. W. (1987) *Gender and Power*. London: Sage.

Connell, R. W. (1995) Transformative labour, in M. Ginsburg (ed.) *The Politics of Educators' Work and Lives*. New York: Garland Press.

Cox, B. and Dyson, A. (eds) (1969) *Fight for Education: A Black Paper* and *Black Paper Two*. London: Critical Society Quarterly.

Cox, R. W. (1980) Social forces, states and world orders, *Millennium: Journal of International Studies*, 10(2): 126–55.

Dale, R. (1981) Education and the capitalist state, in M. Apple (ed.) *Economic and Cultural Reproduction in Education*. London: Routledge and Kegan Paul.

Dale, R. (1986) *Perspectives on Policy-making* (Module 1 of E333, Policy-making in Education). Milton Keynes: Open University.

Dale, R. (1989) *The State and Education Policy*. Milton Keynes: Open University Press.

Dale, R. (1992) Recovering from a Pyrrhic victory? Quality, relevance and impact in the sociology of education, in M. Arnot and L. Barton (eds) *Voicing Concerns: Sociological Perspectives on Contemporary Educational Reforms*. Wallingford: Triangle Books.

Dale, R. (1994) Marketing the education market and the polarisation of schooling, in D. Kallos and S. Lindblad (eds) *New Policy Contexts for Education: Sweden and the UK*. Umea: Umea University Press.

Dale, R. and Ozga, J. (1989) Two Hemispheres, both New Right? in B. Lingard and P. Porter (eds) *Reforming Education in Hard Times*. London: Falmer Press.

David, M., West, A. and Ribbins, J. (1994) *Mother's Intuition: Choosing Secondary Schools*. London: Falmer Press.

Davies, B. (1992) The concept of agency: a feminist post-structural analysis, *Social Analysis*, 30: 179–212.

Deem, R. and Ozga, J. (1997) Women managing for diversity in the post-modern world, in C. Marshall (ed.) *Feminist Critical Policy Analysis*. London: Falmer Press.

DES (1992) *The Initial Training of Teachers*. London: HMSO, Circular 91–92.

Dewey, J. (1916) *Education and Democracy*. New York: Ann Arbor.

Dewey, J. (1966) *Selected Educational Writings*. London: Heinemann.

DfEE (1997a) *Excellence in Schools*. London: The Stationery Office.

DfEE (1997b) *Teaching: High Status, High Standards*. London: DfEE.

Dye, T. (1981) *Understanding Public Policy*. Englewood Cliffs, NJ: Prentice Hall.

Dunleavy, P. and O'Leary, B. (1987) *Theories of the State: The Politics of Liberal Democracy*. London: Macmillan.

Echols, F., McPherson, A. and Willms, D. (1990) Parental choice in Scotland, *Journal of Education Policy*, 5: 207–23.

Edwards, T., Fitz, J. and Whitty, G. (1989) *The State and Private Education: An Evaluation of the Assisted Places Scheme*. Lewes: Falmer Press.

Etzioni, A. (1988) *The Moral Dimension: Towards a New Economics*. New York: Free Press.

Ferraroti, F. (1990) *Time, Memory and Society*. New York: Greenwood Press.

Finch, J. (1984) It's great to have someone to talk to: the ethics and politics of interviewing women, in C. Bell and H. Roberts (eds) *Social Researching: Politics, Problems and Practice*. London: Routledge and Kegan Paul.

Gewirtz, S. (1995) Choice, equity and control in education. Paper presented to the Second Comparative Education Policy Seminar, Sweden and England, Umea University.

Gewirtz, S., Ball, S. and Bowe, R. (1995) *Markets, Choice and Equity in Education*. Buckingham: Open University Press.

Gewirtz, S. and Ozga, J. (1990) Partnership, pluralism and education policy: a reassessment, *Journal of Education Policy*, 5(1): 37–48.

Gewirtz, S. and Ozga, J. (1994) Interviewing the education policy elite, in G. Walford (ed.) *Researching the Powerful in Education*. London: UCL Press.

Glaser, H. and Strauss, P. (1967) *The Discovery of Grounded Theory*. Chicago: Aldine.

Glass, D. and Smith, W. (1979) Meta-analysis of research on class size and achievement, *Educational Evaluation and Policy Analysis*, 1(1): 2–26.

Goldstein, H. (1998) *How Can We Evaluate Educational Research?* London: Institute of Education.

Goodwin, E. and Le Grand, J. (1987) *Not Only the Poor: The Middle Class and Welfare*. London: Allen and Unwin.

Gosden, P. (1976) *Education in the Second World War*. London: Methuen.

Gosden, P. and Sharp, P. (1978) *The Development of an Education Service*. Oxford: Martin Robertson.

Gouldner, A. (1971) *The Coming Crisis in Western Sociology*. London: Heinemann.

Grace, G. (1985) Judging teachers: the social and political contexts of teacher evaluation, *British Journal of the Sociology of Education*, 6(1): 3–17.

Grace, G. (1987) Teachers and the state, in M. Lawn and G. Grace (eds) *Teachers: The Culture and Politics of Work*. London: Falmer Press.

Grace, G. (1989) Education: Commodity or Public Good?, *British Journal of Educational Studies*, 37(3): 207–21.

Gramsci, A. (1971) *Selections from the Prison Notebooks*. London: Lawrence and Wishart.

Granovetter, M. (1992) Economic institutions as social constructions: a framework for analysis, *Acta Sociologica*, 35: 3–11.

Green, A. (1985) *Education and State Formation*. London: Macmillan.

Green, A. (1989) *Education and State Formation*. London: Macmillan.

Habermas, J. (1971) *Towards a Rational Society*. London: Heinemann.

Habermas, J. (1972) *Knowledge and Human Interests*. London: Heinemann.

Habermas, J. (1974) *Theory and Practice*. London: Heinemann.

Habermas, J. (1984) *The Theory of Communicative Action: Vol. I Reason and the Rationalization of Society*. Boston: Beacon Press.

Habermas, J. (1990) *Moral Consciousness and Communicative Action*. Cambridge: Polity Press.

Halpin, D. and Fitz, J. (1990) Researching grant-maintained schools, *Journal of Education Policy*, 5(2): 167–80.

Halsey, A., Heath, A. and Ridge, J. (1990) *Origins and Destinations: Family, Class and Education in Modern Britain*. Oxford: Clarendon Press.

Ham, C. and Hill, P. (1993) *Policy-making in the Modern Capitalist State*. London: Harvester Wheatsheaf.

Hannon, P. (1998) An ecological perspective on educational research, in J. Rudduck and D. Mcintyre (eds) *Educational Research: The Challenge Facing Us*. London: Paul Chapman.

Hanushek, M. (1986) The economics of schooling: production and efficiency in public schools, *Journal of Economic Literature*, 24: 1141–77.

Hargreaves, D. (1994) *The Mosaic of Learning*. London: Demos.

Hargreaves, D. (1996) Teaching as a research-based profession: possibilities and prospects, Teacher Training Agency Annual Lecture, University of Cambridge Department of Education.

Harvey, L. (1990) *Critical Social Research*. London: Unwin Hyman.

Hatcher, R. and Troyna, B. (1994) The 'policy cycle': a Ball by Ball account, *Journal of Education Policy*, 9(2): 155–71.

Hegarty, S. (1998) On the purposes of research, BERA Internet Conference, Paper C, March.

Henry, M. (1993) What is policy? A response to Stephen Ball, *Discourse*, 4(1): 102–5.

Hillage, J., Pearson, R., Anderson, A. and Tomkin, P. (1998) *Excellence in Research in Schools, London*. London: The Stationery Office.

Hood, C. (1991) *The New Public Management*. London: Routledge.

Howell, D. (1990) Some thoughts on researching grant-maintained schools, *Journal of Education Policy*, 5(3): 242–4.

Humm, M. (ed.) (1992) *Feminisms: A Reader*. London: Harvester.

Hutton, W. (1995) *The State We're In*. London: Jonathan Cape.

Jensen, T. (1998) Stress in the Primary School, *The Guardian*, 11 May.

Johnson, R. (1989) Thatcherism and English education: breaking the mould or confirming the pattern?, *History of Education*, 18(2): 91–121.

Jonathon, R. (1990) State education service or prisoner's dilemma?, *Education Philosophy and Theory*, 22(1).

Kemmis, S. (1994) 'Emancipatory aspirations in a post-modern era'. Keynote address to the conference Curriculum Change in Hong Kong: the Needs of the New Era, Chinese University of Hong Kong, April.

Kenway, J. (1992) Feminist theories of the state: 'to be or not to be?' in M. Muctzalgeldt (ed.) *Society, State and Politics in Australia*. Sydney: Pluto Press.

Kenway, J (ed.) (1994) *Economising Education: The Post-Fordist Directions*. Geelong: Deakin University Press.

Kenway, J., Willis, S., Blackmore, J. and Rennie, L. (1994) Making hope practical rather than despair convincing, *British Journal of the Sociology of Education*, 15(2): 102–211.

Lauder, H., Hughes, D., Watson, S., Simiyu, I., Strathdee, R. and Weslander, S. (1995) *Trading in Futures: The Nature of Educational Markets in New Zealand*. Wellington: Victoria University.

Lauder, H., Hughes, D., Weslander, S., Thropp, M., McGlen, J., Watson, S. and Dupris, A. (1994) *The Creation of Market Competition for Education in New Zealand*. Wellington: Victoria University.

Law, J. (1995) *Organizing Modernity*. Cambridge: Polity Press.

Lawn, M. (1987) *Servants of the State: The Contested Control of Teaching*. Lewes: Falmer Press.

Lawn, M. (1997) *Modern Times: Work, Professionalism and Citizenship in Teaching*. London: Falmer Press.

Lawn, M. and Grace, G. (eds) (1987) *Teachers: The Nature and Politics of Work*. Lewes: Falmer Press.

Levačić, R. (1992) The LEA and its schools, in G. Wallace (ed.) *Local Management of Schools: Research and Experience*. Clevedon: Multilingual Matters.

Levačić, R. and Woods, P. (1994) New forms of financial co-operation, in S. Ranson and J. Tomlinson (eds) *Autonomy and Interdependence in the New Governance of Education*. London: Longman.

Lowe, R. (1988) *Education in the Post-War Years*. London: Routledge.

McCulloch, G. (1988) The Norwood Report and the Secondary School Curriculum, *History of Education Review*, 17(2): 30–7.

McIntyre, D. (1998) The usefulness of educational research, in J. Rudduck and D. McIntyre (eds) *Educational Research: The Challenge Facing Us*. London: Paul Chapman.

McLennan, G. (1989) *Marxism, Pluralism and Beyond*. London: Sage.

McLure, S. (1985) *Education Development and School Building*. London: Longman.

McNay, I. and Ozga, J. (eds) (1985) *Education Policy-making: The Breakdown of Consensus?* Oxford: Pergamon Press.

McPherson, A. and Raab, C. (1988) *Governing Education*. Edinburgh: Edinburgh University Press.

Mahony, P. (1997) Talking heads: feminist perspectives on public sector reforms in teacher education, *Discourse*, 18(1): 87–103.

Mahony, P. and Hextall, I. (1997) Teaching in the managerial state. Paper presented to Australian Education Research Association Annual Conference, Queensland, November.

Marginson, S. (1993) Education Research and Education Policy, *Review of Australian Research in Education*, 2: 15–29.

Marshall, C. (ed.) (1997) *Feminist Critical Policy Analysis*. London: Falmer Press.

Marx, K. (1967) *Capital, Volume 1*. Harmondsworth: Penguin.

May, T. (1997) *Social Research*. Buckingham: Open University Press.

Menter, I., Muschamp, Y., Nicholls, P. and Ozga, J., with Pollard, A. (1997) *Work and Identity in the Primary School: a Post Fordist Analysis*. Buckingham: Open University Press.

Middlemas, K. (1979) *Politics in Industrial Society*. London: Deutsch.

Miller, D. (1989) *Market, State and Community: Theoretical Foundations of Market Socialism*. Oxford: Clarendon.

Millet, A. (1996) *Chief Executive's Annual Lecture*. London: TTA.

Millet, A. (1998) Pedagogy and professionalism. Paper presented to TES and Keele Improving Schools Network seminar, Keele University, June.

Mingione, E. (1991) *Fragmented Societies: A Sociology of Economic Life Beyond the Market Paradigm*. Oxford: Blackwell.

Mishra, R. (1990) *The Welfare State in Capitalist Society*. London: Harvester.

Mishra, R. (1997) *Society and Social Policy*. London: Macmillan.

Moore, D. and Davenport, S. (1990) Choice the new improved sorting machine, in W. Boyd and H. Halberg (eds) *Choice in Education: Potential and Problems*. Berkeley: McCutchan.

Moore, R. (1996) Back to the future: the problems of change and possibilities of advance in the sociology of education, *British Journal of the Sociology of Education*, 17: 145–63.

Nixon, J. (1995) Teaching as a profession of values, in J. Smyth (ed.) *Critical Discourses on Teacher Development*. London: Cassell.

Offe, C. (1985) *Disorganized Capitalism*. Cambridge: Polity Press.

Offe, C. (1996) *Modernity and the State: East, West*. Cambridge: Polity Press.

Outhwaite, W. (1996) *The Habermas Reader*. Cambridge and Oxford: Polity Press in association with Blackwell.

Ozga, J. (1987) Studying education through the lives of the policy-makers, in L. Barton and S. Walker (eds) *Changing Policies, Changing Teachers*. Lewes: Falmer Press.

Ozga, J. (1990) Policy research and policy theory: a comment on Fitz and Halpin, *Journal of Education Policy*, 5(4): 359–62.

Ozga, J. and Deem, R. (1996) Carrying the burden of transformation. Paper presented to the European Education Research Association Conference, Seville, November.

Ozga, J. and Gewirtz, S. (1994) Sex, lies and audiotape: interviewing the education policy elite, in D. Halpin and B. Troyna (eds) *Researching Education Policy: Ethical and Methodological Issues*. Lewes: Falmer Press.

Ozga, J. and Lawn, M. (1981) *Teachers, Professionalism and Class*. Lewes: Falmer Press.

Ozga, J. and Lawn, M. (1988) Schoolwork: Interpreting the labour process of teaching, *British Journal of Sociology of Education*, 9(3): 323–36.

Poulantzas, N. (1976) *Classes in Contemporary Capitalism*. London: New Left Books.

Power, S. (1993) The detail and the bigger picture: the use of state-centred theory in researching education policy and practice, *International Studies in the Sociology of Education*, 6(3): 77–92.

Pusey, M. (1991) *Economic Rationalism in Canberra: a Nation Building State Changes Its Mind*. Cambridge: Cambridge University Press.

Ranson, S. (1985) Contradictions in the government of educational change, *Political Studies*, 33(1): 16–25.

Ranson, S. (1988) From 1944 to 1988: education, citizenship and democracy, *Local Government Studies*, 14(1): 1–9.

Ranson, S. (1990) From 1944 to 1988: education, citizenship and democracy, in M. Flude and H. Hammer (eds) *The Education Reform Act 1988*. London: Falmer Press.

Ranson, S. and Tomlinson, J. (1986) *The Government of Education*. London: Routledge.

Readings, W. (1997) *The University in Ruins*. Cambridge, MA: Harvard University Press.

Reynolds, D. (1998) The highly reliable leader. Paper presented to TES and Keele Improving Schools Network seminar, Keele University, June.

Rose, N. (1996) The death of the Social? Re-figuring the territory of government, *Economy and Society*, 25(3): 327–55.

Savage, G. (1983) Social Class and Social Policy: the Civil Service and Secondary Education in England, *Journal of Contemporary History*, (18): 31–9.

Seddon, T. (1996) The principle of choice in policy research, *Journal of Education Policy*, 2(2): 200–14.

Seifert, R. (1987) *Teacher Militancy*. Lewes: Falmer Press.

Self, P. (1993) *Econocrats and the Policy Process*. London: Macmillan.

Sikes, P. (1997) *Parents Who Teach: Stories from Home and from School*. Cassell: London.

Silver, H. (1983) *Education as History*. London: Macmillan.

Simon, D. (1986) The 1944 Education Act: a Conservative Measure?, *History of Education*, 15(1): 5–10.

Soucek, V. (1994) Flexible education and new standards of communicative competence, in J. Kenway (ed.) *Economising Education: The Post-Fordist Directions*. Geelong: Deakin University Press.

Soucek, V. (1995) Flexible education and new standards of communicative competence, in J. Kenway (ed.) *Economising Education: The Post-Fordist Directions*. Geelong: Deakin University Press.

Stanley, L. and Wise, E. (1993) *Breaking Out Again*. London: Routledge.

Tawney, R. (1938) *Equality*. London: Unwin.

Taylor-Gooby, P. and Dale, J. (1981) *Social Theory and Social Welfare*. London: Edward Arnold.

Tooley, J. (1996) *Education without the State*. London: Institute of Economic Affairs.

Tooley, J. (1997) On school choice and social class: a response to Ball, Bowe and Gewirtz, *British Journal of the Sociology of Education*, 18(2): 217–31.

Tooley, J. and Darby, D. (1998) *Educational Research: A Critique*. London: HMSO.

Tropp, A. (1957) *The School Teachers*. London: Allen and Unwin.

Troyna, B. (1994) Critical social research and education policy, *British Journal of Educational Studies*, 42(1): 52–71.

Wallace, M. and Pocklington, K. (1998) Slipping through the cracks: policy literature and implementation of school reorganization initiatives. Paper presented to the American Educational Research Association Conference, San Diego, 13–17 April.

Weaver, T. (1979) *The Control of Education in Britain* (Unit 2 E222). Milton Keynes: Open University Press.

Weiner, G. (1996) *Feminisms in Education*. Buckingham: Open University Press.

Weinstock, A. (1976) I blame the teachers, *Times Educational Supplement*, 23 January.

Whitty, G., Edwards, T. and Gewirtz, S. (1993) Researching a policy in progress, *Research Papers in Education*, 6(2): 3–47.

Wildavsky, A. (1979) Speaking Truth to Power: The Art and Craft of Policy Analysis. Boston: Little Brown.

Willms, J. D. and Echols, F. (1992) Alert and inert clients: the Scottish experience of parental choice of schools, *Economics of Education Review*, 11: 339–50.

Woods, P. and Bagley, C. (1996) Market elements in a public service: an analytical model for studying education policy, *Journal of Education Policy*, (11)6: 641–55.

Yeatman, A. (1990) *Femocrats, Bureaucrats, Technocrats*. Sydney: Allen and Unwin.

Index